Rethinking Childhood

D0234867

Other books in the *New Childhoods* series

Rethinking Children's Communication, Alison Clark
Rethinking Children and Families, Nick Frost
Rethinking Children's Rights, Phil Jones and Sue Welch
Rethinking Children and Research, Mary Kellett
Rethinking Children, Violence and Safeguarding, Lorraine Radford

Also available from Continuum

Promoting Children's Well-Being, Andrew Burrell, Jeni Riley and Ted Wragg
Respecting Childhood, Tim Loreman
Right to Childhoods, Dimitra Hartas
A Sociology of Educating, Roland Meighan, Clive Harber, Len Barton, Iram Siraj-Blatchford and Stephen Walker
Thinking Children, Claire Cassidy
Whose Childhood Is It, Richard Eke, Helen Butcher and Mandy Lee
Working Together for Children, Gary Walker

Rethinking Childhood

Attitudes in contemporary society

Phil Jones

New Childhoods Series

continuum

This book is dedicated to Kyveli Karagiourgou-Short,
Nicholas Karagiourgou-Short, Lola Miller,
Piper Miller, Pavlos Nowak and Zoe Nowak

With thanks to staff and students,
Childhood Studies, Leeds Metropolitan University

Continuum International Publishing Group

The Tower Building   80 Maiden Lane, Suite 704
11 York Road   New York
London SE1 7NX   NY 10038

www.continuumbooks.com

British Library Cataloguing-in-Publication Data
A catalogue record for this book is available from the British Library.

ISBN: 9780826499363 (paperback)

Library of Congress Cataloging-in-Publication Data
A catalog record of this book is available from the Library of Congress.

Typeset by Newgen Imaging Systems Pvt Ltd, Chennai
Printed and bound in Great Britain by
CPI Antony Rowe, Chippenham, Wiltshire

Contents

Introduction to New Childhoods series

The amount of current attention given to children and to childhood is unprecedented. Recent years have seen the agreement of new international conventions, national bodies established, and waves of regional and local initiatives all concerning children.

This rapid pace has been set by many things: from children themselves, from adults working with children, from governments and global bodies. Injustice, dissatisfaction, new ideas and raw needs are fuelling change. Within and, often, leading the movement is research. From the work of multinational corporations designed to reach into the minds of children and the pockets of parents, through to charity-driven initiatives aiming to challenge the forces that situate children in extreme poverty, a massive amount of energy is expended on research relating to children and their lives. This attention is not all benign. Research can be seen as original investigation undertaken in order to gain knowledge and understanding through a systematic and rigorous process of critical enquiry, examining 'even the most commonplace assumption' (Kellett, 2005, 9). As Kellett has pointed out, the findings can be used negatively by the media to saturate and accost, rather than support, under-12s who are described as obese, for example, or to stigmatize young people by the use of statistics. However, research can also play a role in investigating, enquiring, communicating and understanding. Recent years have seen innovations in the focus of research, as political moves that challenge the ways in which children have been silenced and excluded result in the emergence of previously unseen pictures of children's experiences of poverty, family life and community. The attitudes, opinions and lived experiences of children are being given air, and one of the themes within this book concerns the opportunities and challenges this is creating. As this series will reveal, research is being used to set new agendas, to challenge ways of living and working that oppress, harm or limit children. It is also being used to test preconceptions and long-held beliefs about children's lived experiences, the actual *effects* rather than the adult's *opinions* of the way parents see and relate to their children, or the actual impact of services and their ways of working with children.

In addition to the *focus* of research, innovations are being made in the *way* research is conceived and carried out. Its role in children's lives is changing. In the past much research treated children as objects: research was done on them, with the agenda and framework set purely by adults. New work is emerging where children create the way research is conceived and carried out. Children act as researchers, researchers work with questions formulated by children or work with children in new ways driven by a rights perspective.

This series aims to offer access to some of the challenges, discoveries and work-in-progress of contemporary research. The terms 'child' and 'childhood' are used within the series in line with Article 1 of the United Nations Convention on the Rights of the Child which defines 'children' as persons up to the age of eighteen. The books offer opportunities to engage with emerging ideas, questions and practices. They will help those studying childhood, or living and working with children to become familiar with challenging work, to engage with findings and to reflect on their own ideas, experiences and ways of practising.

Dr. Phil Jones
Leeds Metropolitan University
completed Makweti, South Africa
November 2008

Part 1
Debates, Dilemmas and Challenges: an introduction to attitudes towards children

Introduction

Introduction and key questions

In recent times we have seen the growth of new kinds of attention to childhood. Radical questions are challenging long-held attitudes and beliefs about children. The impetus for change is energetic and powerful. This chapter looks at the ways attitudes towards children are changing and introduces some of the key questions and themes within the book.

- How is childhood changing?
- What is research revealing about attitudes towards children?
- What are the uses of looking at attitudes towards children?

How is childhood changing?

The ways that adults relate to children and the ways that children see themselves are being questioned by challenges that are coming from children, lobbying groups, service providers, researchers and parents. From the home to the hospital, from the playground to the web, arenas of children's lives are undergoing change, and are being tested and developed by new thinking, new ideas about practice and new directions in research. Legislation and action within organizations from international bodies to local schools are creating repercussions in all dimensions of children's lives. This change in attitudes towards childhood is expressed by the United Nations Convention on the Rights of the Child (UNCRC, 1989), ratified by all nations except Somalia and the United States of America.

One of the key ideas producing change is the premise that different forces present in many societies are silencing children. Such forces have made children invisible, or rendered them visible only in particular ways. Children are, for example, often seen by adults in terms of stereotypes based on them being incapable or untrustworthy, vulnerable and dependent. This book will review how adult ways of seeing children are contributing to this silencing. It will look at how these attitudes are being challenged and changed.

Another key idea is one that is at the heart of the UNCRC and is summarized by Hill and Tisdall as the view that children are active, engaged participants in their lives and in society, as 'social actors with their own views and goals, and not just objects or problems' (1997, 28). They quote a child asserting

that children should have 'the rights of agency: to take part in family decisions, rights to make our own decisions about our future, rights to live our own life and not what our parents want us to do, the right to our own opinion' (Children's Rights Development Unit, 1994, 24 quoted in Hill and Tisdall, 1997). The change in attitude and practice involves seeing children in their own right and as having rights, not as proto-adults or as the property of parents.

These ideas are the drivers of the contemporary re-examination of attitudes concerning children.

From Eureka! The National Children's Museum, UK

In many arenas of society, in many countries, research is at the forefront of the challenge, the new interest in children's lives and experiences. This research often reveals the difficulty and challenge of being a child, and the ways in which societies are creating adverse conditions for children to be in. The impetus, as expressed by the UN Convention, has formed new questions, and the research reviewed in this book can be seen as energized by them. Table 1.1 (see page 8) takes key elements from each of the guiding principles of the Convention (1989) and links them to the kinds of questions examined in this book and the research it draws on.

Criticism has identified ambiguities, tensions and omissions within the UN Convention. This includes its lack of enforceability unless it is incorporated through national law; the lack of promotion of children's participation through political rights; that definitions – such as that of the child's 'best interests' – may be made by adults rather than involving children's own ideas and agency and that it does not pay attention to the ways in which forces such as patriarchy within society and families affect children. These critiques can also be seen to form the agenda for enquiry and research (see Table 1.2, page 9).

Such challenge and research is creating a different kind of attention towards childhood, and is demanding access for children to be seen and heard in new ways. This emergence of children's voices and experiences has led to issues being acknowledged that were not previously visible. It is revealing pictures previously unseen or repressed: from abuse in the home to homophobic bullying in the playground. The attention to children being seen and listened to in their own right, rather than as part of the family, or through the filter of their parents or carers, is giving new insights into the ways areas as varied as poverty, healthcare or racism are featuring in their lives. This different visibility is creating pictures that demand response.

What is research revealing about attitudes towards children?

Attitudes have been defined in a number of ways. The main focus within the book is on adult's attitudes towards children, children's own attitudes towards themselves, and the interaction between the two. Adults feature powerfully in children's lives in many ways: as parents and carers, friends, providers of services such as schooling or healthcare, members of the community they live within and as legislators. Such attitudes are present in the home

Table 1.1 UN Convention on the Rights of the Child – Principles and Research Questions

UN Convention on The Rights of the Child	Questions
***Guiding principle:* Non-discrimination**	
Children must be treated without discrimination of any kind, irrespective of race, colour, sex, language, religion or other status. (Article 2)	How does discrimination particularly affect children? How can discrimination against children be ended? What are children's experiences of discrimination and how do they challenge it?
***Guiding principle:* Best interests of the child**	
In all actions concerning children, whether undertaken by public or private social welfare institutions, courts of law, administrative authorities or legislative bodies, the best interests of the child shall be a primary consideration. (Article 3)	What does acting in the best interest of the child mean? What is the relationship between adults' perceptions of the best interests of children and children's own perceptions of their own best interests?
***Guiding principle:* Survival and Development**	
States recognize that every child has the right to life and that states shall ensure, to the maximum extent possible, the survival and development of each child. (Article 6)	What forces affect children's survival and development? What ideas about what children should develop into are fuelling adult treatment of children? What are children's ideas and experiences of forces that affect their survival and development?
***Guiding principle:* Participation**	
States shall assure to the child who is capable of forming his or her own views the right to express those views; of the child's views being given due weight in accordance with the age and maturity of the child. The child shall, in particular, be provided with the opportunity to be heard in any judicial and administrative proceedings affecting the child, either directly, or through a representative or an appropriate body, in a manner consistent with the procedural rules of national law. (Article 12)	How does society define when children are old or mature enough to express valid views? What is the relationship between adult attitudes and children's experiences of holding views, participating in decision making and having decisions listened to and acted on? How are children being heard within arenas such as the justice and administrative systems that they encounter?

and in the law court, in the way adults talk to children and the ways policies govern their lives. Given this position, it becomes clear that adult attitudes can have significant positive and negative influences and effects on children's lives.

Table 1.2 Critiques of the UN Convention on the Rights of the Child and Research Questions

Critique of the UN Convention on The Rights of the Child	Questions
The lack of promotion of children's participation in terms of political rights.	How can children be involved in political processes in national and local governance?
Does not pay attention to discriminatory forces such as patriarchy.	How do issues such as gender discrimination and patriarchy affect children? How can such forces be opposed?
Children's rights in relation to areas such as participation are often interpreted as reflecting Westernized concepts that see individuals as autonomous, emphasizing rights such as individual choice. Other cultural ideas which emphasize social co-operation or the centrality of community are often left out.	How can different cultural concepts be reflected in ways of looking at children's rights?

Source: Drawn from Badham (2004), Childwatch (2006), Moss (2002)

The importance of this area can be seen in different ways. Literature on childhood, as well as the directions and findings of research involving children, has emphasized issues concerning power and the nature of the impact of adult attitude on children's lives. The attitudes of adults, in all their different roles and relationships, affect children deeply. Research often concerns itself with identifying problematic issues and using these to identify ways to resolve them. The approach towards attitudes within this book will be to focus on discoveries about ways of identifying and understanding areas where adult attitudes towards children prove problematic. The different chapters aim to try to gain insight into these, and to draw on ideas and research that looks towards ways of achieving change to benefit both children and adults.

In addition, research is revealing that children are not passive in the face of the impact of adults on their lives. This book will also explore how children see themselves and how they view childhood, and examine their responses to adult attitudes. Madge's (2006) survey of over 2000 UK children aged between 7 and 13, for example, revealed aspects of what children's experience of living with adult attitudes is like. The analysis of the children's responses to the questionnaires indicated that they considered the 'worst things' about being a child were restrictions, school and not being taken seriously.

The attitudes of researchers will also be looked at, including interviews with some of the researchers whose work is included in this book.

What are the uses of looking at attitudes towards children?

A number of authors and researchers have pointed to adult attitudes as a key barrier to the development and future of children's lives. It has become fashionable within some societies to talk about children's participation being valuable in developing children's services or policies, for example. In relation to children being able to participate in the creation of policies that affect them, many people have noted that the rhetoric of adults is often not accompanied by actual action to see children and young people's decisions acted upon (Badham, 2004). Adult attitudes that children cannot be trusted as having valuable opinions worthy of being acted on can still stop their real involvement. Criticisms in different countries echo this: that adult attitudes are the 'greatest barrier' to effective participation in areas such as decision making (Bessell, 2007a, 1). These attitudes include:

- perceptions of children's capacities that see them as incapable;
- the idea that children are best served by adult judgements and opinions;
- the idea that adult perceptions about children's lives are more valid than those of children themselves;
- concerns that children will harm themselves, or others, if not governed by adult decision making;
- the confining and restricting effects that stereotyping can have;
- unwillingness to adapt or change processes to enable children's participation;
- a desire to maintain authority over children.

Bessell (2007b) quotes McNeish who says that 'a failure to acknowledge the beliefs and assumptions about children's competency and vulnerability is likely to exacerbate the hidden barriers to participation' (McNeish, 1999, 193). Others have indicated the importance of identifying the ways in which such negative attitudes towards children connect with processes of social exclusion and inequality. They argue that poverty or discrimination, for example, deepen the 'lack of status and respect afforded to children and young people' (ESCR collective paper, 2004, 101).

There is not one narrative of attitudes within this book, as that would not reflect the picture that research creates. Rather, the book attempts to identify key tensions within current attitudes towards childhood in a number of countries. Chapters 2 and 3 give an overview of the developments and set the scene regarding the nature of contemporary attitudes towards children. Thorne summarizes the situation succinctly:

> Until recent decades, children were silenced, their voices unheard and their experiences largely concealed . . . Critical perspectives on the marginalization of children were inspired by earlier political movements on behalf of other subordinated groups such as colonized peoples, racial–ethnic minorities and women. These movements challenged the contours of traditional knowledge . . . These critical approaches helped open attention to the silencing of children and to the goal of bringing them to voice. The theme of 'voice' – voicing experiences, claiming the right not only to speak but also to be listened to – has become a metaphor for political recognition, self-determination and full presence in knowledge.
>
> (Thorne, 2002, 251)

This metaphor, of a challenging, emerging voice that demands to be heard and acted on, runs through much of the research and thinking within this book. This book creates a review of that challenge.

There are many directions that this book could have taken. It looks at a handful of areas as exemplifying some of these key issues within contemporary debates and research, stretching from national policies to family life. The following identifies some of the concerns and questions that the book will focus upon.

Chapter 4 considers the issue of *capability*. Here attitudes concern the ways in which ideas of childishness and the childlike create a vicious circle of expectation and response.

- Do adults encourage the idea of children as incapable and incompetent?
- What are effective ways of recognizing children's capability?

Chapter 5 considers the nature of *stereotyping* within attitudes. This can take many forms within childhood. The key area of gender is focused on as an example of the kinds of ways adult and child attitudes connect to stop and hinder children's development.

- What is the impact of the ways adults try to gender children's worlds?
- How do children respond to their gendered world? How do they make their worlds in terms of gender and image?

Chapter 6 concerns a dynamic present within many societies that of *fear for, and fear of, children*. Here the way adult attitudes affect areas of children's lives from the home to the law court are examined.

- What does research reveal about attitudes towards ideas and practices concerning the protection of children?
- What does research reveal about attitudes towards ideas and practices concerning our fear of children?

The area of *participation* is one that has recently seen an enormous amount of adult attention. The tension between rhetoric and actual action is looked at in Chapter 7. The chapter examines whether children's views are being listened to and acted on, or whether adult attitudes give lip service to consulting children, while keeping actual decision making and true involvement away from them.

- What does research reveal about the impact of adult decision making on children's lives?
- What does research reveal about ideas and practices concerning children's participation in decision making?

Chapter 8 draws together the book's examination of the findings of these kinds of questions, to offer new ideas and practices for changing attitudes towards childhood and the lives children can lead.

The scene painted by this book is one in which changes in attitude are occurring, and where societies are learning more about childhood in ways that they had previously not been able to. The book's approach will be to explore different spheres of children's lives and to identify and examine attitudes towards children. It will consider attitudes that have a negative impact on children's lives and identify

Young Refugee from UK LEAP project (The UK's LEAP Gallery, copyright and permission from The Children's Society. LEAP works to promote the inclusion of disabled children, and refugee and asylum-seeking young people.)

those that are creating positive effects on children. The approach to research is one that draws on work that asks challenging questions about children's lives and the ways adults and children react and relate to each other. The key aim is to make these findings accessible – to help ask questions about adult attitudes and to see how thought, research and practice involving children is offering a changing picture. It will look at how these pictures can produce change for children and can improve their lives.

Part 2
An Interdisciplinary Overview of Recent Research and Scholarship

What are Attitudes Towards Children? 2

Chapter outline

Introduction and key questions

There have been many ways of describing and analysing childhood. Within different cultures and across different time periods there have been a variety of ideas and concepts concerning the state of human development and experience that we currently name 'childhood'. These occur through a dynamic interplay between spoken and unspoken assumptions about what children are and are not, what they may and may not do, how adults can and cannot act in relation to them. This chapter looks at the challenges to traditional views such as that children are innocent, or passive and incapable. It examines new ideas and practices that see children as competent and active agents in their lives.

- Are children still seen and not heard?
- Is childhood changing?
- What are contemporary tensions in childhood?
- What are emerging ideas about 'new childhoods'?

Are children still seen and not heard?

The rhetoric of much adult attention to childhood creates it as a time when many societies like to perceive children as 'care free' or innocent. The picture fed back by research creates very different accounts of childhood. UNICEF, for example, refers to its recent findings as a 'shadow' on this traditional image: 'making the time of life that adults like to think of as happy and carefree into a time of anxiety and misery' (2007, 32). This shadow is linked to the exclusion and deprivation – both material and emotional – faced daily by many children. A key element of this is the way in which adult actions and perceptions, fuelled by their attitudes towards childhood, silence and exclude children. The chapters in this book will explore the different effects of this silencing and exclusion of children.

The UNICEF Young Voices Poll in 2000–01 surveyed children's experiences through interviews with 15,200 children between the ages of 9 and 17 years in over thirty-five countries. Many of the negative findings relate to adult attitudes and ways of relating to children. It reported that sixty per cent said that they faced violence or aggressive behaviour such as shouting and hitting, with 11 per cent saying that it occurred often. When asked about 'rights' for children, more than a third spontaneously mentioned the right not to be hurt or mistreated as being important, with the same percentage saying they felt that this right was not respected in their country. Sixty-one per cent said that their views were not sufficiently taken into account, or not considered at all by local government (UNICEF 2001). UNICEF commented that 'Unhappy children do not thrive, emotionally or intellectually, find it difficult to contribute to a society they believe has given them nothing and risk spiralling towards self-destructive or anti-social behaviour' (2001).

Its 2007 (UNICEF 2007) report on child well-being looked at different dimensions of children's lives such as their material situation, health, safety or family and peer relationships. It painted a varied picture, with the Netherlands and Sweden being ranked as the best overall in the selected dimensions, and the United Kingdom and United States in the bottom third of rankings for five of the six dimensions and being placed as the worst places for child well-being. Poverty, unemployment and deprivation were all highlighted as factors affecting child well-being, as well as related areas such as 'circumstances, pressures and self-perceptions that undermine well-being . . . problems and pressures facing a significant proportion of young people' (2007, 27). Bullying, fighting and abuse varied in different societies – with 15 per cent reporting bullying in

Sweden compared to 40 per cent in Switzerland, Austria and Portugal (2007, 32). The report commented on these factors as creating long-term damage to the development and well-being of millions of children. As a response to the United Nation's Violence Study, the Children's Rights Alliance and National Society for the Prevention of Cruelty to Children comment on the lives of children in many countries being typified by poor housing, physical assault, sexual abuse, neglect, violence falsely legitimized by being described as 'corporal punishment', incarceration because they are perceived to be 'young offenders' or they are seeking refuge or asylum and bullying – 'disproportionately' experienced if they are from a minority ethnic group or are perceived to be lesbian, gay or disabled (2007, 12).

Example of research: undermining children's well-being – the impact of silencing and exclusion

The UK's Children Society instigated the 'Good Childhood Enquiry' with responses from over 13,000 children about their experiences. In one of the documents summarizing the findings for children, a sample quotation identifies an aspect which came up in many of the accounts:

> Bullying is a big problem and some of you think teachers don't do enough to stop it: 'I wish they would deal with bullying better and not say: "stop telling tales".'
>
> (Children's Society, 2007, 4)

A different contemporary survey of more than 6,000 children, involved the largest-ever study of self-harm among 15- and 16-year-olds in England (Hawton et al. 2006). Previous estimates for the amount self-harm in the country were based on the 25,000 'presentations' at hospitals in England and Wales each year that are the result of deliberate self-poisoning or self-injury amongst teenagers. The new research indicates that this was a significant underestimation of the real extent of the problem, with only 13 per cent of self-harming incidents reported by the pupils resulting in a hospital visit. The real figure revealed that 11 per cent of all girls and 3 per cent of all boys reported that they had self-harmed within the previous year. The survey found that girls are four times more likely to have engaged in deliberate self-harm compared to boys. Although self-poisoning is the most common form of self-harm reported in hospitals, the study revealed that self-cutting was the more prevalent form of self-harm (64.5 per cent), followed by self-poisoning through overdose (31 per cent). Of those with a history of deliberate self-harm, 20 per cent reported

⇨

Example of research—Cont'd

that no one knew about it and 40 per cent of those who reported thinking about self-harm had not talked to anyone about it or tried to get help. This research uncovers the silence and invisibility that has marked children's lives and the hidden nature of the phenomena that cause such damage to their lives. The research comments on the reasons why boys and girls self-harm as being varied. However, the most frequent motive expressed by both males and females was as a means of coping with distress.

The research findings beg important and general questions about contemporary childhood. Why are children in such distress? This research revealed that official figures massively under-represent the phenomena. Why is their pain largely unseen and unreported? Why are their experiences silenced and invisible?

Self-harm was more common in pupils who had been bullied and was strongly associated with physical and sexual abuse in both sexes. Also, pupils of either sex who had recently been worried about their sexual orientation had relatively higher rates of self-harm.

Over half of both primary and secondary school pupils report that bullying is 'a big problem' or 'quite a problem' in their school (Oliver and Candappa 2003) with over half of children in Year 5 reporting having been recently bullied. Pupils who are disabled or who are lesbian and gay are cited as experiencing particularly high levels of bullying. Research reveals that 82 per cent of children with learning disabilities in the UK are either bullied at school or when they go out in the evening (MENCAP 2006). Research in Ireland (Norman 2004) revealed that 79 per cent of teachers were aware of instances of verbal homophobic bullying, with 16 per cent being aware of physical bullying at their school, and a full 90 per cent saying that their school's anti-bullying policy did not include any reference to lesbian- and gay-related bullying. In the UK a survey of young gay and lesbian people at school showed that up to three-quarters of them had been bullied, that homophobic language is endemic in schools, with teachers often turning a blind eye to it. Of the group, 70 per cent said the bullying had a negative impact on their schoolwork and half had skipped school to avoid bullying (Warwick et al. 2004). Research in Portugal and Scotland has linked bullying to poor health, depression, suicide attempts, limited achievement and the desire to stay on in education (Observatório de Educação 2006; O'Loan et al. 2006).

Reflections on the research

The above research points out that:

- 'Only 13 per cent of self-harming incidents reported by the pupils resulted in a hospital visit.'
- 'Of those with a history of deliberate self-harm, 20 per cent reported that no one knew about it and 40 per cent of those who reported thinking about self-harm had not talked to anyone about it or tried to get help.'

⇨

- 'Homophobic language is endemic in schools, with teachers often turning a blind eye to it.'
- 'a full 90 per cent [of teachers] saying that their school's anti-bullying policy did not include any reference to lesbian- and gay-related bullying'.

Activity

One way of interpreting these findings is to see them as showing that the experiences of children are 'silenced': not heard or acknowledged. There are many factors contributing to this, but how might this interpretation relate to the concept that adult actions and perceptions, fuelled by their attitudes towards childhood, silence and exclude children?

How and why might adult attitudes make it hard for the experiences of the children referred to in the quotes above, to be noticed, acknowledged and responded to?

From Eureka! The National Children's Museum, UK

Is childhood changing?

Researchers have indicated that preconceived views often contain negative views of children that restrict and damage them. Kemshall, for example, comments that young people are often characterized as 'imprudent, irrational and hence vulnerable, by failing to calculate risks properly or to act wisely' (2008, 22). From a historical, cultural perspective such long-held views that see children in certain ways are in conflict with a powerful, emerging set of pictures which oppose tradition and which offer new ideas and opportunities to children and to society. Authors such as Redmond (2008) see the UNCRC as having a dual purpose which connects with the 're-viewing' of such negative pictures and attitudes towards children:

> To extend the fundamental human rights recognized for adults to children, and to challenge the particular forms of exclusion and exploitation they can face.
>
> To call attention to children's particular status with regard to specific interests, entitlements and vulnerabilities.
>
> (Redmond, 2008, 64)

Often citing the UN Convention (1989) as an impetus, a number of countries are introducing laws, policies and practices within areas such as education, health and play which try to engage with some of the tensions created by these new ideas and pictures of children. The ideas offer a challenge to adults within many roles and relationships, and in many spheres of action and activity. These new pictures and ideas work against stereotypes and the assumptions many adults make in their dealings with children.

Ideas about limitations set by adults, based on their ideas of what children can and cannot do, are being questioned. Notions, based automatically on age, that assume children are not able to make decisions are being held up to scrutiny. Practices in arenas as diverse as the law or religion, which suppress children because of preconceptions about them being subordinate to parental interests, are no longer seen to be valid. The idea that childhood should be a time where responsibility is held by others because children are deemed to be innocent, or too immature, or incapable is being challenged:

> I would like to see the age limits completely scrapped, and maturity brought in. As you grow up your age has a stereotype. I'm trying to escape from that stereotype.
>
> Robin, aged 13 (quoted in Alderson, 1993, 9)

MacNaughton et al. (2007), for example, undertook research initiated by the Department of Education and Children's Services of the government of the state of South Australia. Their finding's echo and reinforce the points made by Robin about adult stereotyping regarding age and capability. The research looked at how to consult children aged between 3 and 4 years of age on gender policy in pre-schools. They found that this was possible by finding appropriate ways to communicate with, and to establish the children's ideas and views. They conclude that their case study work reinforces the 'growing body of research evidence that young children are quite capable of expressing their views on things that affect them' (2007, 465).

Key points: constructing childhoods

The idea of childhood as a construction is key to these concepts and changes: it offers new challenges for practice and research with children. Moss and Petrie (2002) have summarized this approach as including the following ideas:

- Childhood is a biological fact, however, the way it is understood and lived is varied.
- This variety is created through interactions between people, and through the kinds of images of children that inform the ways we act.
- There is never only one version of what a child is: different professions, disciplines, communities create particular versions of what children are, or can be, shaped by politics, history and culture.

The tendency within recent academic discussion and within research is to examine such versions, or images of 'childhoods', often described as ways of understanding childhood, as socially constructed. These have been created by analysing social attitudes and practices from different areas: from education to advertising, from policy making to parenting.

These images do not exist on their own: they are not neat, academic parcels. A useful way to consider them is that they are often present together, in different combinations. They are used as a way of challenging the notion that there is only one kind of childhood, and that childhood is fixed. They serve to show that there are different kinds of childhood, that these have changed over time and that they are different between, and within, different societies and cultures. If this is accepted, then it follows that childhood is constructed, and that the construction has changed over time. Childhood, then, can be seen as something that is active, changing and changeable.

What are contemporary tensions in childhood?

These different childhoods are often presented as a series of types of childhood, or of ideas about children. Each one reflects aspects of attitudes towards children and childhood. One way of looking at the images is to see them as describing different aspects of children's lives and identities. Another approach is to see them as being drawn on to help understand tensions and areas of unease within the way children are seen and treated, or ways in which children see themselves and develop their relationships with others and the world around them.

Such tensions, for example, can be seen in policies, or in the ways adults treat children in hospitals or schools. These might be between the child as 'innocent' and the child as 'threat', the child as 'investment' or the child as 'weak' or 'incapable'. This book will include the idea of these images or types of childhoods. However, it will draw especially on the idea of tensions: that the images are not just ways of describing how children are seen, but are dynamic forces which interact. This approach sees children and adults in interaction with each other, reinforcing, controlling, challenging and testing existing images, creating new ones. Research such as that by Radford and Hester illustrates the complexity of such tensions: 'Historically, the needs and rights of children have either been seen to be the same as those of parents or they have been viewed as at odds with the needs and rights of their mothers . . . this is very much the case today where one area of intense conflict, so-called "co-parenting" and preserving a child's contact with separated parents, is increasingly being seen as the major equality and children's rights issue to be confronted by the family courts' (2006, 8).

Looked at in this way issues about children's lives, women's lives and ideas about family, child rights and women's rights are seen as evolving, developing and subject to change and review. Radford and Hester go on to illustrate how issues concerning the way children are viewed by society, and by the law, in such cases do not only relate to the ways children themselves are seen, but also connect to changing societal views on the family, mothering and domestic violence.

Importantly, much of the research described in this book is rooted in the idea that such images and views do not exist in a vacuum. They powerfully affect children's lives, the adults they live with, and the world they live in. They express and interact with different forces in children's lives. The following examples explore the notion of these images not as static categories, but as tensions with children and adults interacting with, and through, them. It also tries to illustrate the lived impact of these images and the attitudes they portray.

These extracts sample more in-depth analysis in later chapters. They illustrate the range of these attitudes and tensions and develop questions that this book explores.

> ## Example of research: children as passive?
> ### Extract from Chapter 5
>
> He asked about wearing girls clothes before and I just said no . . . He likes pink, and I try not to encourage him to like pink just because, you know, he's not a girl . . . There's not that many toys I wouldn't get him, except Barbie.
>
> white, low income, heterosexual mother (Kane, 2006, 160)
>
> Further discussion: pages 86–90.

Here is the idea that adults shape and form children. They channel, direct and govern the way their children develop. Within this talk of the child's desires and interests the mother here, from Kane's (2006) research, has a sense of her guidance contributing to the present and future of the child: an investment in his future as male. Guidance is seen as a part of parenting, but the way this occurs is not neutral. Quotations such as the one above is interesting in terms of the questions it begs. What visions do adults draw on as they raise children? By supplying images for their children what do they hinder, what do they encourage? Should adults do this to children? Are children passive receivers of such efforts to shape and direct their development?

> ## Example of research: children as innocent?
> ### Extract from Chapter 6
>
> The report notes that new media is met by public concern about their impact on society and anxiety leads to 'emotive calls for action' (Livingstone and Bober, 2005, 3). It notes that some link children's use of the internet to 'violent and destructive behaviour in the young' (2005). Concerns also noted were that 'excessive use' by children is at the expense of other activities and family interaction: 'As we increasingly keep our children at home because of fears for their safety outside – in what some see as a "risk-averse culture" – they will play out their developmental drives to socialize and take risks in the digital world' (2005, 3).
>
> Further discussion: pages 114–117.

This extract includes one of the key tensions within contemporary attitudes. The ideas are that a child is innocent and in need of protection but, at the same time, that they can grow into a threat to themselves, to each other, to adults and to adult society at large. Here the tension between these images can be seen. On the one hand the findings express adult anxieties that children need to be kept safe in the home as 'outside' is dangerous – whether in the street, or through the internet impinging on home safety. On the other is the idea that children can become violent and destructive if not managed and governed by adults in particular ways. The ideas beneath such findings are that children are vulnerable and in need of adult protection, and potentially the opposite – they are harmful and dangerous. Why do these ideas exist? What impact do they have on children's lives? Are they built upon factual evidence of danger, or are they the result of adult attitudes not reflected in reality?

Example of research: children as threat?
Extract from Chapter 6

In the UK, 42 per cent believed that half of all crimes were committed by young people. Official statistics suggest that the figure is more likely to be somewhere between 10 and 20 per cent. Two-thirds estimated the percentage of youth crime involving violence at over 40 per cent. Police records of the numbers of young offenders being cautioned or convicted for violent crimes suggest a much lower figure of 20 per cent.

Further discussion: pages 119–128.

Here is a phenomenon common to many societies and which relates to the questions raised from the previous extract. The perception that youths are a threat is at the forefront of attention in politics and in media coverage. The evidence here is echoed in many countries, and it is that adult anxieties are out of proportion to the actual extent of 'youth crime' and are informed by the reinforcement of stereotypes of children as threatening. Why does this tension exist? Is there a relationship between adult preoccupations expressed through our anxiety and fear *for* children and our anxieties and fears *of* children? What part do stereotypes of children as threat play in our society? What is the impact of them on children's lives and on those who live and work with them?

Example of research: children as incapable?
Extract from Chapter 4

A doctor has examined the child and ordered medication. The child's parents have been trying unsuccessfully to get the child to swallow the medication: he refuses, turning his head away. An assistant nurse comes into the room and watches:

> Suddenly she says to the boy, 'Oh, I see, that's what you're doing, then you can come to me.' She lifts up the boy and puts him in her lap. She holds his legs tightly between her knees. She leans the boy back and forces him to take the medication. The mother stands up and helps. Both the mother and father urge the boy to swallow. All three of them are now bent over the boy, who is retching. The assistant nurse says, 'He's retching, but he doesn't have anything to throw up.' Just then the boy vomits.
>
> (2002, 590)

Further discussion: pages 62–64.

Here is the idea that children cannot reason, make judgements for themselves, and that adults need not consult them about what is happening to them. Instead the underlying picture here is of a child who is handled and 'done to' by the adults and by the service he receives. This connects with tensions often found in fields such as the law, or medicine. These concern whether children are able to be involved in decision and actions about their bodies and their health, or whether they are incapable and immature with adults needing to make decisions for them. One of the challenges here is whether adult attitudes serve children's best interests, or whether they make automatic decisions based on preconceptions about children's capabilities?

Children have been treated in different spheres of their lives, from education to medical care by an attitude that is often described as paternalistic. Within this way of looking children are seen as not able to have the capacity to make judgements and to be worthy of consultation about what happens to them. Their experience of health services such as the excerpt above, is one where parents' judgement is seen as the main issue in a child's experience of their health problem. Parallel to this is their experience of education where children are often not deemed to be effective participants in developing and delivering their school's services through schools councils. Here tensions exist between the idea of the childhood as a time when a child is developing capacities and capabilities and the idea that children are incapable or untrustworthy.

Are children incapable or capable? Do adult attitudes encourage and reinforce the image of children as incompetent? How do such attitudes affect their lives?

Example of research: children as invisible?
Extract from Chapter 7

Lee:	Joe
Steve:	Shut up
Family therapist:	But then, Steve didn't want to know. He was kind of 'No way, leave me alone', but then when you
Lee:	I want Joe
Family therapist:	went back he told you
Dad:	Shut up
Family therapist:	When you're upset Nicky, what do you like people to
Lee:	I want to talk to Joe
Family therapist:	do if you're upset? What do you like people to do?
Dad:	He'll talk to you in a minute when he's finished

Further discussion: pages 142–143.

The extract reflects the notion that a child's opinions and participation is not as valued as that of an adult. Within this transcription from a family therapy session, the adults silence the child, Lee, very directly. Through ignoring the child, or directly telling him to shut up, they shut him off. The attention and value of the interaction and space is focused on the adults. This reflects the idea that children are not able to have valuable input. The assumption is that organizations and services are primarily targeted at adults: children are seen to be best served by adult ideas, opinions and experiences. The child in the excerpt is seen to have less status than the adult, and is told to wait and take their turn after adults are ready to allow them space. The actual effect is to render the child invisible, his input is worth less than adults. One way of looking at this attitude sees adulthood as the accepted norm, with children seen primarily in terms of their not yet achieving this 'normal' state of maturity. Qvortrup summarizes this as seeing children as *becomings*: 'it is the fate of children to be waiting . . . to become adults; to mature; to become competent; to get capabilities;

to acquire rights; to become useful; to have a say in societal matters; to share resources' (2004, 267). This connects with the idea that adults are the valued norm. Children's input is ignored or devalued because of their differences of age, cognitive capability and experience. These are seen as deficits, rather than as a different, valued perspective. Why do adults choose to see children in this way? Are children not capable of opinions and contributions of worth? Are there differences between adult perceptions and contributions and those of children?

What are emerging ideas about 'new childhoods'?

Recent movements have seen the emergence of particular ideas of childhood. They contrast with the kinds of images looked at in the previous section. These are beginning to influence the lives of children. From the ways in which decisions are made in children's lives on a daily basis to broad international policies, common themes have emerged.

This new, or emerging, vision of childhood is not without its opponents and is not without its critics. It can by typified as a new set of specific images of a child and children, and to be associated with the advocacy of certain kinds of relationships and processes. In a way they can be seen to be connected with some of the tensions described earlier.

The core of these as reflected in much recent thinking, practice and research can be summarized as seeing the child as:

- agents in their own lives;
- able to contribute and participate in decision making.

Table 2.1 Emerging and traditional attitudes to children

Emerging view The child as:		Traditional approach The child as:
capable	rather than	incapable
active	rather than	passive
visible	rather than	invisible
powerful	rather than	vulnerable and needy
valued and attended to in the present	rather than	seen and attended to as an investment for the future
an individual with their own capacities	rather than	a mini-adult lacking in full adult capacities

These ideas of children as 'agents' with an emphasis on 'participation' are not to be seen as monolithic concepts with only one way of looking at childhood. They are subject to different interpretations and understandings, and are still evolving. Researchers and practitioners have, for example, pointed out that Western notions of individualism that stress the importance of children being self-determined and having individual choice, which see autonomy and self-esteem as particularly important, may not be a shared way of looking at rights. Differences exist between different communities within countries and between different nations. The Childwatch International Regional Network of Asia Pacific describe:

> country wide studies on the concept of participation in Thailand, China, India, Sri Lanka and Australia. The research has identified a construction of participation as premised on membership of communities or small groups. The western notion of individualism . . . should not prevent us from acknowledging the relevance of alternative constructions . . . that human worth may be rooted in care, inter-dependence and mutual needs.
>
> (2006, 2)

Authors, such as Graham (2007), have rightly indicated the danger of a 'one size fits all' approach to approaching children within this emerging framework. So, for example, attempts to include or involve children must take into account issues such as race and culture and the ways in which other forms of marginalization, children's lived experiences of difference and 'the complex social mechanisms of oppressions that black communities experience' in some societies such as the UK (Graham, 2007, 1307–8). Some have also rightly said that a concern here is that yet another adult-created set of romanticized pictures of children can be seen within this new imagery. This is a danger. However, the direction taken by this new approach may help to resist the replacing of new adult-created images for old. The key act is to emphasize the child's voice or ideas, rather than those imposed on them by adults. The task in much thinking and research involves the act of trying to see how children can increase their participation, to be given a position that engages them as individuals with ideas and opinions. This new vision can be seen to connect to certain emphases:

- Ways of seeing and relating that look at each child as individual rather than through stereotypes of childhood regarding areas such as age and capacity.
- Awareness of the power relations between adults and children and the ways in which this is used to control, manage and to sustain adult perceptions and needs to the detriment of children.

- The formation of relationships with children that aim to empower them rather than to sustain them as reliant and dependent on adults.
- Changing organizations to enable the involvement of children and to ensure their voices are both listened to and acted on.

Connecting the challenging of prejudice based on negative attitudes towards children and childhood to other forms of prejudice is crucial to this empowerment. Authors such as Spring (1994) and Owusu-Bempah (2005) have placed this at the centre of any work with children:

> At the core of an empowering child care practice should be an untiring quest and burning desire to eliminate racial injustice, to promote the well-being of children, regardless of their race, culture, creed, gender or class.
>
> (Owusu-Bempah, 2005, 189)

Within the approach of this book, disability and sexuality can be added to those areas that Owusu-Bempah chooses to include. Connected to this framework to practice are needs in terms of training, approach and attitudes:

- To enable practitioners to be effective and for policy makers to formulate effective policies, any approach to engaging with children should be based in empowerment.
- Education and training should encourage the acquisition of knowledge that transforms taken-for-granted assumptions about the way we currently live.
- Practitioners are empowered to empower the powerless when the practitioner changes their way of thinking.
- This change in awareness is a realization that practitioners can exercise political power within their practice with children and organizations that work with children.
- This power can bring about changes in social and economic conditions (Spring, 1994; Owusu-Bempah, 2005).

This way of re-thinking attitudes and images can be also used to identify an emerging way of creating services for, and with, children. Moss and Petrie, for example, have spoken of 'rethinking public provisions for children' based on who we think children are, what a good childhood consists of and the purpose of services and provision for children (2002, 2). They contrast aspects of current attitudes and provision that are questioned by emerging changes in attitude, with new ideas to be put into practice in services for children.

Common justifications for services are based on:

- children seen as needy, weak and poor – in need of 'rescue and protection';
- the idea that society needs protection from children who are a threat to 'order and progress';

- the child is seen as a 'futurity', as a becoming adult, rather than in terms of their current state;
- the idea that intervention in children, below a certain age, will 'cure all our social and economic ills'.

This is contrasted with provision for children that is based on

- the creation of spaces for children and for the childhoods children are living here and now;
- relationships and solidarities between children;
- creating relationships between adults and between adults and children;
- democratic and ethical ideas and ways of working together with children.

Moss and Petrie acknowledge that some children do need protection, that some can act as a threat and that in certain ways children's present situations will relate to their future lives. However, they critique the current trends towards an emphasis on extensive interventions in children's lives. They link this to it being primarily fuelled by factors such as economics and the prominence of market capitalism in parts of the world. They ask, for example, whether '"social engineering" of children's lives (is) the way to give the modern nation state a competitive edge in the global rat race?' (2002, 3). They formulate questions which relate to issues already cited in this book, concerning our relationship and attitudes towards children and childhood:

- What is the place of children and childhood in our society?
- What is the quality of relationship we wish to promote between children and adults at home, in children's services and in society at large? (2002, 4).

The identification of images and attitudes can help identify the ways in which often negative notions and constructions drive areas such as service provision. These can be used to help us to become aware of the impact of negative assumptions, and to begin to identify ways in which different images and ideas can be brought into play. Moss and Petrie, for example, ask why some societies, such as Britain, 'choose mainly to talk about and portray children in such predominantly negative ways' (2002, 56). They identify a challenge to this in the position within other societies where 'rather than weak, they choose to speak about the child as strong, rich in resources and competent' (2002, 56).

A key action within this challenge is to identify and stop the ways in which adult attitudes restrict and silence children and their participation. If one set of fixing, stereotyping attitudes from adults towards children is replaced with another set that reinforces the power of adults to dominate children, then the work of recent research, thinking and practice will have been for nothing.

From Eureka! The National Children's Museum, UK

Summary

This chapter has

- looked at the ways adult attitudes shape and affect children's experience of childhood;
- examined different approaches to understanding childhood;
- reviewed research that examines ideas and practices concerning the idea of tensions within the way children live and are seen – including children as passive, innocent, threat, incapable and invisible anxieties rather than the actual situations of children and young people;
- looked at the relationship between research that offers insights into children's lives and the emerging ideas of the 'new sociology' of childhood.

Research details

Undermining children's well-being: the impact of silencing and exclusion

Peer-reviewed research. Survey of more than 6,000 children, involved the largest-ever study of self-harm among 15- and 16-year-olds in England (Hawton et al. 2006).

Children as passive

Extract from Chapter 5

Peer-reviewed journal. Questionnaires and interviews were with 42 US parents, mothers and fathers, four being in a married pairs, of children who each had at least one child aged 3 to 5. They were aged 23 to 49 years, including single- and two-parent families and were from a variety of backgrounds and class, racial and ethnic groups including white, Asian American and African American and heterosexual and lesbian and gay parents. The descriptions of background are from the researchers descriptions.

Kane, E. (2006) '"No way my boys are going to be like that!" Parents' responses to children's gender nonconformity', *Gender and Society*, 20, 149–76.

Children as innocent?

Extract from Chapter 6

The research aimed to investigate children and young people's use of the internet, looking at issues concerning risk and opportunity in order to contribute to academic debates and policy development. It was based on a national UK survey conducted face to face with 1511 children and young people aged between 9 and 19 and a survey of 906 of their parents. The research also drew on a number of focus groups and observations of children's use of the internet.

Livingstone, S. and Bober, M. (2005) *UK Children Go Online: final report of key project findings.* London School of Economics and Political Science. LSE Research online.

Children As Threat?

Extract from Chapter 6

Research undertaken by the UK Nuffield Foundation and UK Institute for Criminal Policy Research. Hough and Roberts (2003, 2004) reported on a survey to explore public opinion about youth crime and justice in the UK. It aimed to explore public knowledge of questions relating to this area and attitudes to sentencing young offenders.

Hough, M. and Roberts, J. V. (2003) *Youth Crime and Youth Justice: Public Opinion in England and Wales.* The Nuffield Foundation and the Institute for Criminal Policy Research.

Hough, M. and Roberts, J. V. (2004) *Youth Crime and Youth Justice.* Bristol: The Policy Press.

Children as incapable?

Extract from Chapter 4

The research (Hardy and Armitage, 2002) followed twenty-four children between 5 months to 18 years in a hospital looking at the degree of participation in decisions concerning their own care. Different levels of involvement were agreed and the researchers used these to evaluate 137 individual interactions between child, staff and family.

Hardy, M. and Armitage, G. (2002) 'The child's right to consent to x-ray and imaging investigations: issues of restraint and immobilization from a multidisciplinary perspective', *Journal of Child Healthcare*, 6, 2, 107–19.

Children as invisible?

Extract from Chapter 7

Peer-reviewed Journal. O'Reilly's (2006) research analysed videotapes of a number of different family therapy sessions. This used a qualitative approach to examining the recordings to investigate how children's communications were treated by adults within the therapy sessions. This included looking at both family members' and therapists' ways of interacting with the children in the sessions. The research focused particularly on how children's interruptions were responded to by family members and by the therapists.

O'Reilly, M. (2006) 'Should children be seen and not heard? An examination of how children's interruptions are treated in family therapy', *Discourse Studies*, 8, 549–66.

3 How are Otherness and Childhood Connected?

Introduction and key questions

New questions challenge our existing ideas about what children are, and can be. A key theme in this questioning concerns ideas about 'otherness' and the notion of 'othering'. Othering has been described, at its simplest, as a separation of 'us' and 'them'. This chapter will look at the concept of 'otherness' and the ways in which it relates to adult attitudes towards childhood and children.

- What does being 'other' mean?
- Childish and immature: are children the ultimate other?
- Are children seen primarily in terms of not being adults?
- How does children's otherness affect their lives?
- Can othering be challenged?

What does being 'other' mean?

De Castro has described children as being seen in most spheres of contemporary experience, from the home to national policy making, as being 'other' than adult. Other, in this context, is seen as what is not the same, what is not identical to, or confluent with, the dominant notion of the acceptable self. She has said,

> Difference between children and adults consists . . . of a separation between them which ensures for the child a position of being the one who is not . . . Difference becomes the result of an all-or-nothing quality (or set of attributes) that either child, or adult possesses. Thus conceived, difference between children and adults has served to regulate social (domestic and collective) practices as well as public policies concerning the status of children in our modern societies.
>
> (de Castro, 2004, 470)

These processes are seen to limit children and their lives.

Othering has been described as

- a process that serves to mark and name those who are different from oneself;
- a way of distancing and stigmatizing those who are deemed to be 'different' from a majority, or powerful, group;
- a way of securing one's own identity by distancing others because of perceived differences;
- re-enforcing majority notions of identity, or the self, as normal and that others who do not conform to these 'norms' are to be seen as 'deviant';
- ensuring that people who are seen and identified as 'other' experience being marginalized, disempowered and excluded – this can be through limiting access to areas such as education, or through discrimination in employment, physical access, the removal of rights or using devices such as the law to deny equal status;
- ways of behaving in daily interactions to reinforce outsider status;
- ways of seeing others as in need of being managed, or controlled, by the majority because of their differences or perceived 'deficits' from the 'norm';
- the maintenance of othering requires that 'they' and 'their stories' remain distant and strange or unheard, so that opinions and experiences are not given value, they are silenced and excluded from being heard

(adapted from Spivak, 1985; Bhabha, 1994; Weis, 1995; Grove, 2006).

Looked at in this way, difference and 'deviance' from adult norms are sought out and seen as negative: 'they do what we don't' – children's not being 'the same' as adults is seen as a deficit from the adult state. This 'othering' can create not only distance but also a sense of opposition and conflict, leading to 'us against them'. The 'other' is then often perceived and treated as a threat to the norm rather than as a difference to be welcomed. In turn this is used by the majority to govern or police this difference by treating it as wrong or deviant (Bhabha, 1994).

This chapter will explore further what this 'otherness' and othering of childhood involves: how children's lives are affected. It will examine some aspects of current new thinking and actions that are being developed in response to children as being made to be 'other'.

Childish and immature: are children the ultimate other?

The concept of a certain adult male state being the norm permeates many areas of experience in children's lives. One of the ways this happens is through children's developmental state being seen as a lack or deficit, and in terms of different elements which are inadequate, rather than childhood being seen as having its own attributes and validity. Allied to this is the ways in which the idea of childhood or allied terms such as 'childish' or 'childlike' are seen as 'other' than the desirable or required norm. This is so ingrained that it is seen not just in attitudes towards children, but it is also used towards people in general. The widespread presence of the idea of childhood as signifying inadequacy and the incomplete shows in the negative way we use terms such as 'childish' or 'immature' within many societies.

The use of terms and concepts such as immaturity or incapability is one that is central to the way children are, and have been, treated. Terms such as 'immaturity' have been made to be so synonymous with childhood that we assume they are the same. Contemporary developments in thinking and research challenge this.

It is interesting to look at the ways in which the concept of 'immaturity' is used in many societies. Its use reflects the way that childhood is seen to be an ultimate state of non-participation, of being unacceptable as a valid participant in society: an ultimate 'other.' It can be helpful to see how this use of immature/mature has been used as a tool in the governing of other groups in society. The process of using immaturity to govern difference by inventing a series of 'lacks' related to a state described as being childlike has been used by male majority culture to segregate, disenfranchise and silence different groups and to use that to justify actions as well as to create and uphold social norms and legal situations; for example, women, black and Asian people, lesbians and gay men, people with disabilities. A number of authors have indicated the particularly close relationship between the oppression of women and that of children, given the ways in which in most societies their lives are closely allied.

This 'immaturity', then, is not in itself an actual biological or psychological phenomenon, but is a term, a way of assigning a certain kind of meaning to biological and psychological conditions that occur in the time of life we call childhood. The ways in which ideas about 'immaturity' exist in a society reflect this process of assigning meaning by those who hold social and political power: adults. In the past, and within aspects of a number of contemporary societies, this is often adult, white, able-bodied, heterosexual-identified males. The very word 'immature' asserts the idea that a certain mature state is the norm and 'im' is a lack of this state. Is it possible to say that there is nothing immature about childhood, rather that the use of the term reflects a much wider process that is a way of seeing and making childhood a state that is *lacking*. This process of making it lacking means that certain ideas can be imposed, segregating children from spheres and activities which are said to demand 'maturity'. This maturity is seen to involve decision making, responsibility and the right to have your voice given authority or value. 'Maturity' is also used to exclude children through social practices concerning their voice in family decisions in areas such as divorce, or through the law in areas such as voting, or decisions about their own bodies.

Are children seen primarily in terms of not being adults?

Authors such as Stainton Rogers (2004) have criticized aspects of the impact of influential ideas about child development proposed and regulated within fields such as education and psychology. Here notions such as that of cognitive development describe childhood in terms of different stages in areas such as thinking capacity, or ways of understanding the world and relationships. The critique echoes the earlier consideration of maturity. Such developmental theories are criticized as they position children as 'lacking' adult capacities in terms of autonomy, rationality and responsibility. They see children as psychologically and emotionally dependent, vulnerable and in need of certain experiences and opportunities that, if not given, will undermine the idea of 'proper development' (2004, 130). Babies and young children, for example, have needs and vulnerabilities, but the way in which children are seen by adults has come to emphasize seeing the child as a series of needs, and not as having potentials and capabilities. Stainton Rogers asserts that this way of viewing children extends to later in life and this approach has become ingrained, culturally rooted. It is expressed through fields such as psychology, and 'informs our thinking, the "needs" discourse is applied as much to adolescents as it is to smaller children' (2004, 130). This is linked to society problematizing childhood as a whole: seeing children and young people as lacking, vulnerable and needy but also as inherently troubled and troublesome and, therefore, 'always ever "in need" of adult surveillance, intervention and control' (2004, 130). This, in turn, is seen by Stainton Rogers as a prejudice that influences attitudes and actions between adults and children.

In this way children are described as, and seen to be closely allied to, the idea of the immature. Immaturity becomes seen as a series of deficits, with maturity seen to be a desirable norm that is defined as being like a certain kind of adult masculinity. This idea of normal adulthood becomes rewarded in a number of ways in different spheres of life.

Key points: rewarding the norm

These rewards, of being seen to be the norm in terms of 'maturity', are often seen in law or custom as the capability, or right, to do certain things. Examples are:

- to make decisions about your body in areas such as surgery;
- to develop emotional and sexual relationships;
- to decide what to do in your day;
- to own things and to earn money.

In addition, ideas and attitudes towards the 'norm' mean that individuals who are adult male have been seen to have certain attributes that others are seen not to have, such as:

- to think in ways that are described as rational and that are seen to be an indication of capability;
- to be able to make decisions that are described as 'valid' in areas such as health or the law;
- to have opinions that are listened to, and acted upon.

Being different from this proscribed norm becomes punished by the removal of rights through the law or through custom:

- not to be able make decisions about your body in areas such as surgery, and to need another person to decide for you;
- not to develop emotional and sexual relationships, without the sanction of others;

⇨

- not to decide what to do in your day, this being decided by others and reinforced through legislation or law;
- not to own things and to earn money as you are deemed unfit to do so;
- because the norm of verbal language is not your main means of communication, you are deemed not fit to communicate.

Activity

Hill et al., for example, in their review of UK policy and practice summarize:

> On the one hand, children and young people are enmeshed in policy as passive recipients and arguably oppressed by certain policies. Not only are their weekday activities closely supervised and controlled in school but increasing concern has been expressed in the media and by some politicians about children congregating in their communities.
>
> (2004, 81)

This is a situation that can be analysed as reflecting this 'othering'. How does this process of supervision and control connect with the list of areas listed above in 'removal of rights' and the daily lives of children? Consider how you see the relationship between children and adults at different ages for each category.

How does children's otherness affect their lives?

If this approach to maturity and otherness is accepted then certain questions arise:

- How does it affect children's lives?
- What are children's response to this otherness?
- Are there alternative forces at work and other ways of engaging with childhood?

'Othering' affects children's lives through laws and policies. Cultural practices and organizations are developed to favour and encourage people who fit the profile of the adult norm: through employment, wealth, cultural acceptability. Such practices are also seen to deny access to people who are different, who are 'other' than this. A number of theorists and researchers have linked exclusion with the idea of 'otherness'. Hill et al. (2004), for example, refer to two connected meanings of the term 'social exclusion'. One links to poverty and the ways in which a lack of material sources such as income make it difficult, or impossible, for people to share in the activities generally expected within their society. The other meaning, they say, refers to the ways groups are 'marginalised, omitted or stigmatised' usually because of a difference 'from the majority and which the majority finds hard to accept' (2004, 79). These differences are seen as being 'other' and include gender, race, class, disability, sexuality and age. Pierson has said that the key process in this exclusion is 'grounded in poverty and disadvantage, but works across several dimensions of social life, with lack of access to education and work, weakened social networks and loss of self esteem and influence over events' (2001, 101). These factors can affect children in many ways – because of a child's race, gender or disability. Moss, for example, has shown how the notion of equal treatment for children in relation to services such as education or the law is affected by factors such as their position in relation to race, or being in the family of those seeking political asylum:

> some children's entitlement to equal treatment in relation to service provision has been deliberately removed by the government. Children of asylum seekers who have been denied refugee status face deportation, detention and the threat of removal from loving parents. The rhetoric of Every Child Matters is undermined by this abuse of their human rights.
>
> (2008b, 50)

However, across all kinds of childhood the idea is that children face particular kinds of exclusion and othering in terms of their status as children.

Key points: adult attitudes as the greatest barriers

Hill et al. state that adult perceptions are the 'foremost barriers to participation' and inclusion. They see these perceptions as:

- images of children's capacities;
- adult self-interest in maintaining their own position with respect to children;
- a view of children's rights as undermining adults' authority and rights;
- a zero-assumption that transferring responsibility to children invariably takes something away from children;
- a fear that children will exercise their rights in an irresponsible and self-centred way;
- children being consulted on children's issues but not considered to hold any valid representation on adults issues (2004, 83).

Key within a number of treatments of these areas of exclusion and othering is the concept of power and power relations. Tomlinson, for example, draws attention to the ways in which othering has implications for decisions on a macro level. There is a 'differential political status' between children and adults in many democracies. Macroeconomic policy and practice, for example, largely ignores children's needs and wants:

> The crux of the question is how we transform political and economic agendas to put at their centre concepts of children as citizens, to consider and respond to their interests and needs and further their well-being. In some countries, such as Canada and South America, all policy decisions have to be measured against potential outcomes for children.
>
> (Tomlinson, 2008, 37)

That this is not the case in countries such as the UK or USA, where this othering can be identified, and is reflected on a large policy-wide economic level. Children are not automatically seen within the central concerns and processes of decision making.

Can othering be challenged?

Much of the emerging focus since the 1990s has seen an emphasis within many countries on the challenging of this othering. This has occurred within many spheres of children's lives and in the ways adults live and work with them. Welch (2008) notes this growth and locates it in three main areas designed to promote children's rights:

- to provision;
- to protection;
- to participation.

Hill et al. note that within this growth, however, 'many social exclusion policies are directed at young children, yet their voice is rarely heard' (2004, 82). They note a shift towards the concept of the participation by children and young people being valued as a normative principle.

Material such as UNICEF and Save the Children's *The Evolving Capacities of the Child* (Lansdown, 2005) reflects a 'rights based approach' to the 'evolving capacities' of the child and the creating of environments to promote and respect children. These offer a challenge to theory and practice that silences and makes the child 'other'. For example, Moss refers to Cannella and Viruru in discussing otherness and children. He talks about the importance of listening and consulting children, but acknowledges that this is a complex process. Listening and consulting must take account of power relations and their inequalities between adults and children:

> When voice is 'conferred' upon 'the other' . . . without recognising or attempting to alter the inequities that created the original distinctions, the 'giving of voice' or 'listening to' just becomes another colonising apparatus.
>
> (Cannella and Viruru in Moss, 2005, 12)

Another view champions the idea of children's 'difference'. The idea is that children's otherness, their difference, offers a challenge to adult-orientated norms of identity, and contemporary ideas about key areas of social and cultural experience such as education, play, work and decision making. Ideas that connect to this notion range from a rights perspective and ideas of adultism to current fashions of 'child centredness' (Wright, 2001).

This book will draw upon specific illustrations from research into policy and children's lives including their experiences of services. It will be used to examine the concept of child centredness and the importance of involving the child's voice. Approaches to understanding and responding to adult attitudes that create children as 'other' will be examined; for example, 'behaviours and attitudes based on the assumption that adults are better than young people without their agreement . . . This mistreatment is reinforced by social institutions, laws, customs and attitudes' (Bell, 1997). This book will explore the ways in which such concepts can have an impact through a re-examination of the role and nature of children and childhood, and on policies, services and relationships with children.

Summary

This chapter has:

- looked at the ways adult attitudes see children in terms of their being 'other' than adults;
- examined different approaches to understanding the effect on children of being seen in terms of 'other' than adults;
- reviewed ideas and practices that challenge this way of seeing children of viewing childhood;
- looked at the idea that childhood is a state in its own right, rather than a time typified by inadequacy and incapability.

Part 3
Implications for Children's Lives

Incomplete Adults? Decision Making and Autonomy

4

Introduction and key questions

This chapter focuses on the ways in which children's competency is seen. It will examine adult attitudes and practices that treat children as incomplete or imperfect adults, and those that see the child as competent in their own right.

The chapter will draw on research to challenge practices that disempower children by treating them as incapable, and that excludes them from decision making by assuming that they are not competent.

- What is an incompetent child?
- Do adults encourage the idea that children are incapable and incompetent?
- What is a competent child?

- Maturation, dependency and autonomy: old enough to make a decision?
- Can children be trusted? Children and adult power
- What are effective ways of recognizing children's capability?

What is an incompetent child?

How competent are children? Ideas and practices concerning, for example, the ways in which children are seen as dependent upon adults are reflections of a combination of inherited and newly generated beliefs and adult needs. Adults argue, or simply assume, that children are most effectively served by adult figures such as parents or doctors making decisions for them. One of the terms often used is that they act in the child's 'best interest'. The central idea of this chapter is that, often, it is not children's interests but adult interests that are best served by adults making decisions for children.

This chapter will show how adult attitudes that children are not capable have been so strongly held that:

- adults have created a world for children that constantly reinforces the preconception that children are not competent;
- adults have convinced themselves that it is beneficial for children that adults rather than they make decisions. Rather than as malign control, the way adults see this is as 'care' or 'protection' in the 'best interests' of the child.

The ways that those working and living with children see, and think they see, what children can and cannot do have recently been questioned. The idea is that fields such as education, biology and psychology have framed questions and created ways of looking at children that are wrong. They do not *actually* see what children are like or what they are capable of. Their conclusions are often flawed because the questions they ask about children are based in preconceptions based on adult ideas and beliefs. These ideas are that children are typified as being incapable, irrational, vulnerable and needy. The status of children's competence evokes strong feelings and responses. An editorial in the *British Medical Journal*, for example, framed issues of competence and consent in the following way:

> In all but the most life threatening circumstances it amounts to an abuse of a child's rights as a member of society to disregard a refusal to consent to treatment if the child seems to have made a fully informed and considered decision. This is especially true . . . with the classic family unit having so often disintegrated; the child may have a more stable and balanced viewpoint than either parent.
>
> (Shield and Baum, 1994, 1182)

This challenges the idea of parental views being assumed to have more value than a child's because they are more competent or credible. In addition, it states that refusal to permit a child to be seen as a competent decision maker on their own bodies and treatment is a form of abuse. The following examples from different parts of the world give a sense of the range of the areas of children's lives that are being re-examined in research and enquiry. Here we see competency as an issue in giving witness in legal situations; in decisions about family arrangements after divorce; in making policies at national level; and in making decisions about the school curriculum. The research in each case is informed by the kinds of questions that, until recently, would not have been asked in many parts of the world, as existing attitudes would not have seen them as relevant.

Table 4.1 Previously held beliefs and new questions

Previously held belief or attitude	Children were not competent to tell right from wrong, or truth from lies in the courtroom.
New question	Can children as young as five be deemed capable of taking an informed oath?
Origin of research	US research into 4- to 7-year-old children's competence to take oath (Lyon, 1995).
Previously held belief or attitude	Children are not able to make valid judgements in family life crises such as a divorce, and need protection not involvement.
New question	Are children capable of being involved in decisions about their family's future?
Origin of research	Child participation in decision making regarding arrangements in cases of parental divorce in the Netherlands and the UK (Hemrica and Heyting, 2004).
Previously held belief or attitude	Children are too naive and have too little experience of life to make political judgements.
New question	Are children competent to make valid judgements about national policy making?
Origin of research	Competency in involvement in national policy making in Brazil (Kirkby and Bryson, 2002).
Previously held belief or attitude	Children are not capable of having any input into the curriculum they are taught, or in reflecting on staff or the way the school is managed.
New question	Are children capable of reflecting on their education and formulating and making valid suggestions about the content and process of their schooling?
Origin of research	Competency in involvement in school councils and in curriculum decision making in schools in Denmark, Germany, the Netherlands and Sweden (Davis and Kirkpatrick, 2000).

The answer in the cited research relating to each of these 'new' questions, put at its simplest, was 'yes'. In each case this 'yes' involves adults and children re-examining long-held attitudes towards the relationships formed between adult and child concerning competency.

Often existing policies and practices are framed within the idea of the 'best interests' of the child. A number of theorists and researchers, however, have pointed out that in reality this idea of best interest is often carried out by adult organizations and individuals 'self-policing', and that 'the best interests of the child are sometimes dictated by our own attitudes and beliefs' as adults rather than through 'considered interaction with children' and on the basis of any actual evidence (Hardy and Armitage, 2002, 116). Current thinking has started to ask questions, and to call into doubt, long-held beliefs about the 'incapacity' of children and their 'best interests' being served by adult perceptions or decisions made for them by adults.

Best interests?

The contemporary take is that adults or parents act 'in the best interest' of the child. Most would frown at the image we often give ourselves of a Victorian attitude of 'children should be seen and not heard'. The contemporary idea in many societies is that children are loved, attended to, protected by parents and professionals alike who think of them, regard them and make decisions about them. The phrase in 'the best interest' often occurs in policies and in the law in relation to this process of adults deciding for children. This attitude permeates areas such as education, health and democracy in local or national decisions: from the family to the state, from adults making decisions about a child's operation to voting in elections 'on behalf of' their interests. In reality, though, the practice and impact of contemporary attitudes is often deeply parallel to the Victorian 'seen and not heard' attitude. Children have been resolutely silenced from decisions about their bodies, their education, the life of their family in processes such as divorce, and in government decisions about areas as diverse as play and protection.

The way this concept of 'best interest' can simply erase and exclude children may be seen beneath the text in this extract from the US *Journal of Contemporary Law and Policy*:

> As with incompetent adults, the physician himself owes duties to the child patient himself and those duties in some circumstances require resisting or even refusing

surrogate's choices. Those duties may be conceptualized as requiring medical professionals to ensure that parents are making the same decision that the child would make if able to do so, or as requiring medical professionals to ensure that parental choices are consistent with what objectively is in the child's best interests. In other words, the professional obligation owed to a child patient is the same as that owed an incompetent adult patient.

(Svoboda et al., 2000, 61)

Within this framework on US law the child is not deemed capable in any way, and is seen as parallel to those adults who are labelled 'incompetent'. There is an automatic assumption that the child cannot make decisions. Professionals act upon a set of further adult-based assumptions: there is no notion of trying to perceive, or imagine, what the child would decide on from their perspective as a child. Rather, the professionals are to regulate, or 'ensure', that parents arrive at a decision defined by the adult professionals themselves. Even though the word 'choice' is used, there is no mention of supporting parents and child in reviewing and assisting in a decision based on alternatives. Hence medical workers make sure parents arrive at the 'right decision', defined as 'objective' by professionals. The idea that the child as patient should be involved in being made aware of choices concerning their body is not visible in any way within this legal, medical, adult way of seeing children. The child is erased, except as the object of adult decisions and judgements.

In their review of papers on policy concerning children presented at a UK ESRC seminar in 2004 Hill et al. summarize a key theme:

many measures introduced ostensibly for children's benefit have subsequently or currently proved to be harmful or questionable, whether we consider sending children to the colonies in the 1960s or the failings of child welfare and protection systems today. The current policy concentration on children 'at risk' and the 'poor child' . . . masks the subordination/exclusion of all children.

(2004, 81)

As with the *British Medical Journal* cited earlier, this commentary questions the assumed validity of adult decisions and ideas about childhood and children's lives. This mirrors the idea that adult-created policies and practices however seemingly well-intentioned, may well suit adult ends and goals, but actually act to silence and mistreat children.

Do adults encourage the idea that children are incapable and incompetent?

One of the common ways of seeing the period which we name as 'childhood' is that it is a time of maturation and growth, where needs for food and shelter cannot be fully met by the individual without support, and a time where cognitive and emotional development occurs. The idea of competence in childhood is varied and ambivalent. It has been defined from a number of different perspectives in relation to this time of maturation, need and development. These vary from ideas of competency in social and cultural spheres, to those in use within legal and medical contexts. Social competence takes phenomena such as problem-solving behaviour, perspective taking and effective social interaction, and perceives them as criteria for seeing a child as competent. In legal and medical provision, areas are negotiated and proscribed by policies and laws concerning issues such as adult perceptions about a child's competency to decide about a medical procedure. Weare and Gray note the diversity of meanings given to 'children's competency' with a 'wide range of terminology in use in the field' (2003, 6). As this chapter will show, an aspect of this diversity reflects an uneasy and shifting attitude within many societies to children and competency. These ideas about children's competency have become intertwined with particular ways in which adults respond to, and frame, them. France, for example, has argued that 'the young are seen as being in a "stage of deficit", where they lack morality, skills and responsibility' (2007, 152). The ideas have become associated with powerful adult definitions often associated with negative images of children. The definitions are through language, attitudes and ways of behaving.

Adult attitudes and the vicious circle of incompetency

These definitions regulate and participate in the ways in which adults see and treat children, and in the ways children see themselves. They define adult–child relationships and the services provided by organizations surrounding the processes or growth, need and maturation of children. As elsewhere in this book, this chapter reflects the view that these can seem fixed, whereas they are constructions largely made by adults. These constructions are currently under question, and this section will examine the dominant beliefs about children in relation to issues such as competency and the growth and maturation they experience. It will look at the ways in which research is challenging aspects of traditional ways of dealing with children's perceived and actual 'competence' and 'incompetence'.

One of the central emerging ideas is that adults, often unconsciously, prepare children to be dependent upon them. How do adults encourage children to see themselves in this way?

- Through creating laws that confine children.
- Through creating policies that confirm adults' attitudes that children need adults to make decisions for them.
- Through interacting with each other, and with children, in ways that do not allow children to express themselves or to participate in decision making.
- By using adulthood as a measure that is set as a norm against which other states, such as childhood, are seen as lacking, or in terms of being a deficit.
- By seeing and treating children as incapable and inadequate.

This preparation can be seen to create a vicious circle for children. Adults have a framework within which children are raised and responded to. This framework sees and treats them as not capable. One of the effects of this is that children's own expectations and ways of seeing themselves are constructed within this incapability. In turn, the way they behave reflects this, which fulfils and confirms adult expectations. This can create situations that are unhelpful and harmful. Bluebond-Langner (1978), in her research with terminally ill children, found that children as young as three years of age were aware of their diagnosis and prognosis without ever having been informed by an adult. The research discovered that adult attitudes seeing children as being not competent to handle this information, and in need of 'protection' against it, led to the child feeling abandoned and unloved. The research pointed out that at the same time, the child's response was often to 'protect' the 'unaware' adults, despite great personal cost (Bluebond-Langner, 1978).

If adult attitudes and the reality of children were confluent, then the situation would be static. There would be no need or occasion for tension, challenge and change. However, the rise of different attitudes from children and young people, and within sections of the population of adults who live and work with children, has created change. In the UK, for example, a series of decisions and counter-decisions regarding the notion of children's competence have occurred. One of the key arenas concerns health-related practices in areas such as medical, dental and surgical treatment. In the UK, from a legal challenge, the notion of the 'Gillick competent' child has arisen.

> Unlike 16- or 17-year-olds, children under 16 are not automatically presumed to be legally competent to make decisions about their healthcare. However, the courts have stated that under 16s will be competent to give valid consent to a particular intervention if they have 'sufficient understanding and intelligence to enable him or her to understand fully what is proposed' (sometimes known as 'Gillick competence'). In other words, there is no specific age when a child becomes competent to consent to treatment: it depends both on the child and on the seriousness and complexity of the treatment being proposed.
>
> (DoH, 2001a)

These views of children affect different aspects of their lives and are treated elsewhere in this book. They connect to the way children are subordinated, the way children relate to the world they live in. Within this chapter the focus will be on how these ways of looking relate to competency and decision making.

Key points: children as incapable

- Children as not able to make valid or worthwhile decisions about their lives.
- Children as incomplete adults.
- Childhood as a stage in becoming.
- Children as unreliable.
- Children as a threat.

Each of these can be seen reflected in the ways adult attitudes have informed policies which emphasize and reinforce such views of children in the law, policy and guidelines for professional practice, However, they are challenged and new attitudes are emerging.

What is a competent child?

Such attitudes have been challenged by the rise of a critique of these ideas of children. The critique points to the presence of ways of looking or framing children as described above, and offers a different approach to children's competence. The alternate view is often set up as a series of oppositional views. The following is a more specific version of the table produced in Chapter 2:

Table 4.2 Traditional and emerging positions

Traditional position	Emerging position
Incapable	Capable
Not able to make valuable decisions	Active decision-makers with opinions that matter and making decisions of worth
Incomplete adults	Seen in terms of own capacities, not in terms of deficits or deficiencies based on the idea of adult functioning as the norm
As a threat to themselves and others due to deficits in reasoning and experience	As able to contribute usefully

This emerging position is not without its challenges and difficulties. The issue of how competence and capability can be defined and seen is complex. The situations within which issues of capability arise also raises questions: Does a child have different competencies in relation to different spheres of their lives? How is competency to be involved in family decision making to be compared to making decisions needing to be made in medical contexts? Questions arise out of the issue of differences regarding capability: How is the issue of age regarded? How do we view differences arising from personality, such as shyness, or from learning disability, class or ethnicity? Are such questions irrelevant if you view the child from a point of view that sees them as capable, and that stresses their right to make decisions about their own, and others, lives?

The following discussions and research illustrates aspects of the ways children and adults encounter the 'traditional position' and examines the issues identified here in the emerging position that emphasises the child as competent and capable.

Maturation, dependency and autonomy: old enough to make a decision?

There is confusion between biological issues such as a child needing to be fed and given shelter, or that they are developing, and adult concepts and practices that define *how* their needs are seen and met and *how* their development occurs. The idea is that this is used by adults to keep children in a state where they are seen to be so incapable that adults must make decisions for them.

As noted in Chapter 2, the UN Convention on the Rights of the Child says in Article 12 that states will assure to the child who is 'capable' of forming their views that they are given the right to express their views in matters that affect them. The nature of competence here is left open, however, in relation to issues such as chronological age and factors such as poverty or disability that arise through social exclusion.

Some research has linked the issue of competence and age to issues regarding participation and social inclusion.

Example of research: children, divorce and separation

Research by Mantle et al. (2006) looked at the issue of the 'age of the child' regarding welfare reports made in the context of divorce and separation by CAFCASS practitioners (Children and Family Court Advisory Service). These reports are made by practitioners working with the children. Those writing reports are obliged to establish the child's wishes and feelings. The involvement of children in mediation in such situations, as well as parents and carers, is an emerging area of practice. The research involved reviewing data of 1586 children who are the subject of welfare reports and in-depth interviews with twelve law practitioners. The children were spread across different ages: 25 per cent aged 4 or under, 42 per cent aged 5 to 9 and 32 per cent aged 10 and over. The researchers noted that within emerging practice, professionals 'make a number of assumptions about the child's competence based on chronological age' (2006, 499).

The research explored the issue of the age of the child in particular. However, the researchers link together three concepts, which they propose are of enormous power in emerging practice in this area:

- The capacity of the child to contribute, whatever their age.
- The right of the child to be involved.
- Their uniqueness.

The idea being that the issue of age cannot be isolated, but needs to be seen in relation to these additional factors.

Approaches are often seen to be rooted in common assumptions about what is possible given a child's age. They cite the way CAFCASS differentiates its information to different age groups (BMRB, 2004) or divisions such as those proposed by McNamee et al.:

- At less than 5 years old the child is not seen 'to be considered "old" enough to talk' (2003, 171) and that this 'lack' is assumed to lessen the capability of the child.

⇨

- At 5–9 years 'children can talk and be listened to' but practitioners will not automatically give weight to what is being said.
- At 13 year and above, what children say is often listened to and given 'weight' (2003, 171).

This is contrasted with the idea that practitioners take what they call a stance of 'uncertainty' this is typified as:

- treating each child as unique;
- avoiding adult constructions based on age about what the child is capable of and competent to do.

A combination of observation, play and 'direct communication' was used in some of the work (2006, 511). The following is a description from a meeting with an 11-year-old girl.

> A very tall girl so you'd take her possibly for second year of secondary school . . . I'd already observed her going into quite a baby voice and acting very immaturely . . . I let her get down and play and do the funny baby voice for a while, I think it was a form of anxiety because she calmed down and we were able to start to talk about the family situation and, as she got into it, she steadily started to behave more age appropriately, although it took quite a long time.
>
> (2006, 513)

Reflections on the research

The worker does seem to bring concepts of general standards and levels into her commentary. These include judgements about how an 11-year-old should be expressing herself, what behaviour should be in terms of age. In addition, the assumption is that talking is the norm to be arrived at after expression through a baby voice and 'acting very immaturely'. These seem to indicate that the worker has a set of criteria that she uses to judge whether the child has arrived at a point where her views and expressions are to be taken seriously. On the other hand, the worker tries to interpret and understand what is occurring within the relationship – so the voices and acting immaturely are only partially dismissed. They are seen to be part of the child's anxiety and that, as time and relationship move on, the child is seen to 'calm' and to behave in a way that is seen to help focus on the 'family situation'.

The analysis shows how the actual practice of the worker is complex. It combines a mixture of held views reflecting how adults judge and set norms of age appropriateness and maturity, while, at the same time, trying to 'see', 'listen', interact and interpret to locate and report on the child's views and feelings.

⇨

Example of research—Cont'd

Activity

It is interesting to look at this set of comments from the research in terms of the following:

- ideas about maturity and immaturity;
- treating each child as unique;
- concepts of age appropriateness based on adult preconceptions based on age and capability.

How do you see these featuring within, or being absent from, the account?

Stereotyping and age

Hardy and Armitage have argued that stereotyping children 'en masse as lacking the ability to make competent reasoned judgements fails to acknowledge the progressive nature of children's growth, and their increasing capacity for rationality and autonomy' (2002, 112). They link this to the paternalistic attitude adopted to children in healthcare services, for example. Runeson et al. (2007) echo this in their research, saying that, historically, a highly paternalistic and medically dominated view of patients prevailed in healthcare, and this has been exacerbated in the situation of children. The ladder of participation originally proposed by Arnstein and subsequently adapted by Hart (1992) for use with children is an idea expressed by various models working to move from paternalism, and to try to provide a structure to assist in taking action about participation. The UK's Royal College of Paediatricians and Child Health, in its four levels of participation, includes competency as a key issue. As well as listening and taking account of their views so they can 'influence' decisions it talks of: 'respecting the competent child as the main decider about proposed healthcare interventions' (2002, 584).

Researchers have examined the state of practice in healthcare regarding children and the way they are treated as a result of adult attitudes. Research has looked, for example, at the issue of the restraint or immobilizing of children in hospitals, specifically in relation to x-ray. They define restraint as restriction to which consent has not been given (Hardy and Armitage, 2002, 111). In relation to medical treatment of children, where radiographic examinations are undertaken, the research notes that many are carried out by radiographers without formal paediatric education or training (2002, 108) and that choice and permission were problematic areas in terms of children being seen as competent to decide what was to happen to them. Hardy and Armitrage (2002) make a direct comparison between the position of adults and children. Under law, adults have the right to refuse consent to medical treatment, and, in the absence of consent, action being taken in the 'best interests' of the patient would not be a valid defence. The law regulating consent and children differs from country to country. They note that in situations such as that in the UK, there is high ambivalence regarding decisions made by or for children. The document 'Seeking Consent: working with children' (DoH, 2001a) for professionals practising within the UK's Department of Health locates decisions in the hands of adults in the following way:

> If a child of 16 or 17 is not competent to take a particular decision, then a person with parental responsibility can take that decision for them, although the child should still be involved as much as possible. However, once children reach the age of 18, no one else can take decisions on their behalf.

Examples of being 'not competent' include a child being in pain or fatigued, or under the influence of medication side effects. The notion of incompetence is based on notions of capacity and competence:

> You should never automatically assume that a child with learning disabilities is not competent to take his or her own decisions: many children will be competent if information is presented in an appropriate way and they are supported through the decision-making process.

The information for children is provided in a separate document 'Consent what you have a right to expect – a guide for young' (DoH, 2001b) and says:

> *When can you give consent for yourself?*
>
> Sometimes if you're under 16.
>
> If you are under 16, you may still be able to give consent for yourself provided you're able to understand what is involved in the proposed treatment. . . .
>
> *What if you don't want to consent but your parents do?*
>
> The rules say that your parents may still decide that it is in your best interests to have a particular treatment, and give their consent on your behalf. This rule applies until you reach the age of 18.

The statement to professionals summarizes the situation as being that, 'In other words, there is no specific age when a child becomes competent to consent to treatment: it depends both on the child and on the seriousness and complexity of the treatment being proposed' (DoH, 2001b). Hardy and Armitage's subsequent comments on this draw attention to the fact that there is no objective measurement of this version of 'competence' (2002, 114). They summarize the current UK situation as one of problematically high ambivalence regarding decisions made by, or for, children (2002, 115). This leaves the situation open for adult attitudes to combine with paternalistic approaches. The following research looked at the actual experience of consent for children. It can be seen in relation to how consent and competence can be affected by adult attitudes within this 'ambivalence'.

Example of research: decisions during hospitalization

The research (Hardy and Armitage, 2002) followed twenty-four children between 5 months to 18 years in a hospital looking at the degree of participation in decisions concerning their own care.

Different levels of involvement were agreed. At one end were situations that were characterized by no communication between the children and staff. The researchers typify this as children's integrity not being respected: 'Who had to sit without clothes on the examination table, who had pain or whose wish to be left alone was disregarded, who protested against taking medication' (2002, 590).

At the other end of the measurement, staff act in accordance with the child's opinions, wishes and valuations. In between were stages where staff listen but refuse to discuss the child's opinions with the child with no two-way communication, staff communicating but the child's opinions, wishes and valuations not influencing staff actions, and staff 'caring' about what the child says but acting only partially in accordance with the child's wishes.

The following example is of a 3-year-old boy who has come to hospital with a high fever. His parents have not been able to get him to drink anything, his mouth is open and saliva is trickling down his chin. A doctor has examined the child and ordered medication. The child's parents have been trying unsuccessfully to get the child to swallow the medication: he refuses, turning his head away. An assistant nurse comes into the room and watches:

> Suddenly she says to the boy, 'Oh, I see, that's what you're doing, then you can come to me.' She lifts up the boy and puts him in her lap. She holds his legs tightly between her knees. She leans the boy back and forces him to take the medication. The mother stands up and helps. Both the mother and father urge the boy to swallow. All three of them are now bent over the boy, who

⇨

is retching. The assistant nurse says, 'He's retching, but he doesn't have anything to throw up.' Just then the boy vomits.

(2002, 590)

At the other end of the scale the researchers give as an example a 4-year-old who
is attending hospital for a major operation. The day before the operation the boy is
having breakfast with his mother in his room. A nurse and a children's nurse enter
the room, the boy asks them to leave until after he has had his breakfast, and they
comply (2002, 592).

Other work involved staff listening to children's views, answering their questions,
and is described by the research as staff trying to create a trusting relationship
with children and to motivate the child to take part in the planned procedure – for
example, in preparation for a biopsy of a tumour, inserting an intravenous cannula.
In some situations the research found that in cases where a child had differing opinions from staff, it was often possible to find a compromise. They note that usually
children could not make decisions about the main issue, but could make what is
called 'partial decisions' (2002, 592). More than half of these concerned medical
orders such as taking part in examinations, or samples for tests.

The involvement of children is framed within issues such as age and competence.
The researchers note that 'The child was seldom given time to think about it or ask
questions' and views were not sought. The researchers also note that 'as a rule' a
plan was presented, no alternatives offered. For example, explanations about why
the child was to take premedication were 'seldom given' (2002, 594).

One way of interpreting this is that the child is not seen as an individual who is
capable of decision making or thought, and staff do not interact with, or permit, the
child to behave as if they have the capacity for decision making.

Other situations observed staff making real efforts to create a trusting relationship, attempting to have the child participate in discussion or in the medical procedures. The researchers interpret this as staff working as if 'he or she were a valid
partner whose opinions, wishes and valuations were taken into consideration, and
they did not hurry the procedure' (2002, 594).

Out of the 137 situations observed, the researchers conclude that in sixty-five
cases a child's opinions and wishes were totally or partially respected, and in seventy-two they were not. Factors were identified as involving the protest of the child,
role of parents, attitudes of staff, time and if alternatives within the treatment were
available (2002, 595). They note that parents tend to feel that healthcare staff
'know best', and that they support medical staff in situations where the child's side
could have been heard. The researchers conclude that at times 'parents may also
need to be encouraged to stand back and enable their child's voice to be heard'
(2002, 595). Staff, the conclusion says, often feel that they are presenting the 'best
solutions' instead of offering involvement in thinking about alternatives.

Age was not shown to be an overriding issue. Some practice showed very young children being allowed to participate to a higher degree, and older children being denied.

The research concludes that interactions with children should be undertaken with
a consideration of different perspectives relating to their competence, looking at

⇨

Example of research—Cont'd

how to respect a child's integrity and 'how to balance children's rights of participation with the benefits of medical and nursing interventions', calling for nurses to assess children's competence and investigate their opinions, wishes and values. The research advocate that factors such as a child's comparative confidence or shyness need to be taken into account (2002, 596–7).

Reflections on the research

The emphasis is on the need to recognize the competence of a child, and on critiquing the ways in which practice and service conditions can create situations which mean that staff and parents do not leave opportunities for a child to be involved.

The idea here supports the proposition that adults can create a vicious circle whereby they leave little room for the child to be seen as capable, because their preconception is that children are not capable. The researchers noted that in no situation they observed did a child verbally say they did *not* want any information. They also noted that in some situations children made 'strong protests' and some were moved to expressions described by the researchers as 'totally losing control over the situation and kicking and screaming in panic' (2002, 593). In turn this vicious circle can mean that children are only left room to behave as if they are not capable. This is broken by enquiry and practice which questions such assumptions and practices and which shows ways of fostering a child's capability.

There is no doubt within the article that some medical procedures must be undertaken within healthcare, however. The research is used to advocate the position that, whatever the medical situation, the child should be seen as an active, reflective participant, rather than as incapable and passive.

Activity

Reflect on how you think each of the following recommendations from the research would assist in involving children as competent participants in healthcare:

- Information adapted to children's needs and wishes, different alternatives offered more often.
- Children being given an opportunity to think and ask questions in peace and quiet.
- Children being asked their views on planned interventions (2002, 597).

Can children be trusted? Children and adult power

Another issue often present in relation to capability concerns adult views of children as not to be trusted in relation to their own lives and experiences.

Connected to this is the ways in which, within services, adult opinions, practices and voices can come into collision with those of children. The attitude is often that children's opinions are less trustworthy than adults. Power relations can ensure that children are not heeded: their views identified as invalid or inappropriately biased. Fielding offers the following quotation from an adult US schools board member: 'If students knew how to run the school system, we wouldn't need an administration . . . teachers and principals don't sit on the board, and neither should students'; another saying that 'we can't serve in Congress or as president until we pass age requirements; why should local government forgo the wisdom of this? Students need to learn respect and have life experience before taking a community office' (Joiner, 2003 in Fielding, 2004, 1).

A number of authors such as Fielding (2004) and Raymond (2001) have identified the growth of the idea and practice of pupil involvement in policy circles, nationally and internationally. Tornay-Purta et al. (2001) in *Citizenship and Education in Twenty Eight Countries* places the idea that children can take part in democratic process at the heart of his comments on children's engagement with 'democratic process' at school, and their wider capacity for engagement in what they call civic knowledge and engagement. This presents a very positive view of the capacity of children for valid participation. The UK's DfES 'Working together; giving young people a say' is an example of such attention, with its intention to support embedding pupil participation in school life. The preparation of this initiative involved a consultation group of children, and their statement exemplifies the optimism and goals of this type of involvement:

> We as children and young people know what we want. The only way we can change things is to make sure that people who make decisions know what we think and what we want. If you don't get involved you are more likely to get only what other people want. Knowing what other people's views are leads to making better decisions.
>
> (DfES, 2003 ii)

However, the act of seeking views and giving children the power as competent individuals whose views are taken seriously and acted upon, or negotiated with, by adults is complex.

The following report on research reflects many of these concerns to do with children's capacity to be 'mature' or 'trusted' enough for their views to be taken into account compared to 'mature' and 'trusted' adults. A number of authors have begun to examine the education system in various societies from perspectives that emphasize children's voices as capable commentators of their experiences. Devine's (2002) interviewing of pupils in primary schools in Ireland, for example, revealed the children's perceptions of themselves as subordinates, whose views were not taken seriously. The following research example reflects the ways in which the differences between adult and child decision-making capacities and power can be used by adults as a way of not acknowledging children's opinions and input when it is not what they want to hear.

Example of research: power dynamics and believability

The researchers (Duckett et al., 2008) were approached by a Local Education Authority to help them understand 'children's sense of well-being in school'. This was linked to the UK National Healthy Schools programme introduced in 1999. The LEA had co-opted three local schools to become involved in a research project 'to explore how school demoted and promoted pupil well-being'. The research team framed their approach as 'to gain a rich contextualized understanding of pupils' psychosocial experience of school life and how this was implicated in well-being and explore future ways of working ways of working with the LEA to implement positive social change in those schools' (Duckett et al., 2008, 93). The aims were to explore areas such as the social and emotional well-being of pupils in schools, notions of pupil participation and 'equality and power processes as negotiated between teachers and students' (2008, 93). Pupil comments included:

> It makes me angry that teachers always say this and that about the Bullying Policy but all it is is a thick booklet that they hand out to parents saying how they won't tolerate bullying. But they are useless words on paper. No action is ever taken. (female pupil, written, Year 8)

> People call you (names) . . . It hurts, you get lower and lower by the time you go home you feel like crying. (female pupil, written, Year 8)

> I was in (subject) the other day and the teacher came up to me and pushed me out of the room. So I told him not to push me and then he threatened to suspend me. (male pupil, interview, Year 8)

> (2008, 97)

In chapter 4 of their report, Duckett et al. comment that 'Pupils variously described teachers spreading gossip around the school about pupils, humiliating and making fun of pupils, issuing unwarranted detentions and victimising pupils. Pupils experienced such behaviours as nothing short of brutalising.'

⇨

Miss Shannon (pseudonym), she used to shout at me a lot and she used to make me stay behind . . . she used to pick on me. (Kirsty, interview, Year 8)

When I arrive at school our form gets totally blocked by the form tutor so for the first 20 minutes of school I get someone screaming down my ear. (Written, Year 8)

(Duckett et al, 2004: 69–70)

Following this initial meeting the LEA sought to exert their ownership rights over the research, to limit our involvement in any action that might result from the report and to impose their own right to oversee any attempt by us to publish the findings of our report to a wider audience – such as through journal papers and conference presentations. In spite of these attempts at censure, we managed to persuade the LEA that our child-centric version of the report should distributed to pupils.

(2008, 99)

The full reports were distributed to each school's management team. Delays in meeting with the LEA occurred: 'these delays appear to have reflected the LEA's attempts to come to grips with some of the more contentious findings in our report such as teachers bullying pupils, drug use among pupils, incidents of racism and reported instances of teachers sexually harassing pupils' (2008, 98).

[T]o have diluted our findings even more than we have done so in our reports to the LEA and school pupils would have resulted in us placing increasing levels of adult-centric spin on what we intended to be a child-centric piece of research. However, if the vested interests of children become pitted against the vested interests of adults, then we might find that child-centric research is doomed to failure at worst, or considerable messiness and frustration at best. . . . Obstruction of the school system to research that uncovers findings it deems uncomfortable or threatening is not uncommon.

(2008, 103–4)

Reflections on the research
Activity

How do you see the processes at work within this research relating to:

- the act of seeking views and giving children the power as competent individuals whose views are taken seriously and acted upon, or negotiated with, by adults?
- children's capacity to be 'mature' or 'trusted' enough for their views to be taken into account compared to 'mature' and 'trusted' adults?

Consider the processes from different perspectives: from the experience of the children involved, the school staff, the education authority and the researchers.

Interview with Paul Duckett about the team's research

Paul Duckett, Division of Psychology and Social Change, Manchester Metropolitan University

Phil Jones: How do you see the issue of competency and power in relation to the story of your research?

Paul Duckett: If we take the issue of power first, prior to and during our research we considered issues of child–adult power relations quite extensively and had grounded our work in a theoretical approach that sought to empower the child's position in relation to adults (using Community Psychological and Sociology of Childhood perspectives). We had not, however, fully anticipated how those power relations would be impacted by the adult–adult power relations in our research (specifically, our relationships with the Local Education Authority [LEA]). As such, we fell into the trap that, perhaps, many in the social sciences fall into of seeking to understand power by looking at those who have the least of it (e.g., pupils in a school) rather than at those who have the most of it (e.g., administrators of a school). The focus of our research was to understand well-being at school by exploring the nature of child–child and child–adult relationships. While we were doing so the adult–adult relationships in the background would ultimately determine the extent that the voices of the children in our study would be heard. The power of the local school administrators to prevent us further access to the schools meant our research relationships with the children were severed once our research relationship with the LEA soured (i.e., after we had presented the results of our research to the LEA that showed not all was well in the schools in their area).

Now, to the issue of competence. This concept was largely used by schoolteachers and school administrators to muffle the children's voices. At best, we were warned that the children were incompetent sense-makers (they misunderstood things) and, at worst, we were told the children were incompetent truth-sayers (they lied about things). Such warnings were issued both in anticipation of and in reaction to the children telling us about their negative school experiences. Following our decision not to question the children's competencies in this way, we then had to protect how our own competence was perceived against the charge that we were naïve researchers duped by manipulative children. In this way, competence was: enveloped in power relations; employed to challenge claims over 'truth' and 'knowledge'; and, invoked to protect vested interests (the researchers' right to publish and the teachers' and administrators' right to protect the reputation of their schools).

Phil Jones: What did you discover about the process of researching from this experience?

Paul Duckett: This experience re-affirmed to me the messiness of doing research and the temptation of sanitizing research reporting, but did so in a new way. My answer to this question is not unrelated to the previous question on power and competency. I believe it is again an issue of the adult–adult power relationships and how the perception of competency (both anticipative and reactive) can influence how researchers represent their work to their peer group (through publishing in academic journals, presenting at conferences and so on). In our reporting of our research, we could have provided a much 'neater' account of what we did and used the detail of our methodology (which I believe was innovative and sophisticated) and our findings (which I believe were rich and extensive) to block out the failings of our work. By choosing to write about the problems we encountered, we opened ourselves to being viewed as incompetent and naïve researchers. Indeed, this is how we were viewed by at least one anonymous peer reviewer for a journal where we submitted one of our research papers (our paper was subsequently rejected, though was later accepted by a different journal – the one you have cited in this chapter). In many ways, we were locked into adult-centric notions of competence. As university-based researchers, we were in one educational institution (tertiary education) studying children in another educational institution (secondary education) with both institutions having as their core business the administration and classification of the competence of students. While the use of the concept of competence was not as perniciously invoked against us as adults as it was against the children in our study – our academic peers did not doubt (publicly, at least) our ability to tell the truth, only our ability to find the truth – it may nevertheless have been used by us (in anticipation of how our peers might view our work) and by others (in reaction to how we reported our work) to distort how the findings from our research was disseminated. On reflection, while the Sociology of Childhood alerted us to how children are conceptualized by adults as incompetent, inexperienced, immature and so on, it perhaps did not alert us to how challenging such conceptualizations of childhood can subject you to an infantilizing process whereby your identity becomes rendered similar to how adults render the identity of the child.

In May 2008 the UK's Department of Education produced guidance building on the consultation quoted from earlier. The Department also notes that inspections of schools through Ofsted gives pupils opportunities to 'give views' about their education and links this to support of Article 12 of the

United Nations Convention on the Rights of the Child (UNCRC) and links these actions as a response to children having the right to put forward their views and ensuring that those views are taken seriously, but they note that it is for Local Authorities, teachers and governors to decide how best to involve children and young people. This means that there is no guarantee of the nature and status of such view giving. As this research could be argued to show, adult attitudes can affect the way such processes are engaged with in ways that do not acknowledge children and young people as capable by engaging in dialogue or action with their views (Teachernet, 2008).

What are effective ways of recognizing children's capability?

Some have pointed out that systems such as those of education, the law, child welfare or health are often allied to seeing children as primarily dependent, rather than as seeing them first as capable and independent. Schildkrout has said that adult attitudes depend upon children 'to produce, maintain or ratify adult statuses and relationships – equally as much as children depend upon adults' (1978, 111). This is also attached to other frameworks of power relations such as gender, race, ethnicity, class and kinship. In addition, some have suggested that adults can manipulate children so that their seeming expression of opinion is affected by adult attitudes that frame or exploit children's lack of experience in expressing themselves and being given credit for being able and capable. Researchers have commented that despite efforts to facilitate children's engagement as capable and to make process as child-centred as possible, 'it should be acknowledged that these children are being provided with choices by adults in powerful positions in relation to them, welfare professionals and immediate carers, which may affect their feelings of freedom to make choices' (Holland and O'Neill, 2006, 94).

Some have argued that the idea of broad concepts of children's capability is unhelpful and that attention needs to be given to each individual:

> I would like to see the age limits completely scrapped, and maturity brought in. As you grow up your age has a stereotype. I'm trying to escape from that stereotype.
>
> Robin, aged 13 (quoted in Alderson, 1993, 9)

Others have drawn attention to the way context and capability are important to consider. It is not just about whether a child is given the recognition that they are able to have opinions that are valued: creating appropriate contexts which appreciate factors such as family dynamics, anxieties about the setting or implications of their decisions on their life outside the setting need consideration. Weare and Gray reported in their research conclusions on the importance of including cultural factors in understanding specific children's relationship to competence. They observed that 'what constitutes . . . competence in different cultures will vary greatly' (2003, 78). Factors such as the extent to which a culture values the individual or the collective, and perceives the ways individuals can be autonomous and independent relate to a child's attitude towards themselves as an autonomous decision maker, for example (2003, 78).

Holland and O'Neill's research involved interviewing children and young people regarding their opinions about the process of family conferences and notes young people's accounts of the risks as well as advantages. Family group conferences involve meetings convened by professionals to try to work with a family in order to make 'decisions regarding children' in the field of child welfare, for example (2006, 92). Holland and O'Neill examined young people's opinions about their participation in the process. The priorities of professionals towards enabling the child to have a voice that is recognized as capable might not be shared by service users, including children. Context can be an issue that affects a young person's sense of the desirability of being involved in family group conferences and being seen as a capable contributor on family issues, for example, One of the 16-year-olds, Martine, illustrates this:

> When I got to the place that it was in, all my nerves started kicking in and I thought, here we go, it's just going to be all my family sitting there having a go at me, but when I got in there everything was going to be all right, it was OK.
>
> (2006, 106)

Alderson and Montgomery have challenged the deficit position of children's capability, and proposed the formation and practice of a children's code of practice for healthcare rights that assumes children of compulsory school age are competent. Within this framework healthcare professionals would have to justify ignoring the views of the child (Alderson and Montgomery, 1996).

Some research has explored the ways in which children can be coached to effectively assume the role of a 'health partner' using video, age-appropriate workbooks and role play. The goal was to enable children to raise concerns, ask questions, note information and participate in the creation and troubleshooting of potential problems with the care plan. Coached children preferred an active role in their care and reported better rapport with the physician, recalling significantly greater amounts of information about their medication regimen than controls (77 per cent vs 47 per cent, respectively) (Lewis et al., 1991).

Some research has talked about the importance of creating an environment that encourages and supports children as competent:

> an environment that enhances competence and wellbeing is one that fosters warm relationships, encourages participation, develops pupil and teacher autonomy, and fosters clarity about boundaries, rules and positive expectations.
>
> (Weare and Gray, 2003, 8)

Key points: approaches to capability

What creates such an environment? Key issues and findings within such debates and the research drawn on in this chapter around children's capacity and capability include the following:

- Children's capabilities are best encountered from a basis of assuming capability rather than incapability.
- Age is only one factor to take into account, and other issues such as the arena of the decisions, or issues to be considered, and the individual's experiences and situation are key.
- Adults often assume that a child cannot give consent based on their own preconceptions.
- Capability is connected to the way a situation with a child is created by adults and children working together to maximize their capacity to be involved in decision making.
- Adult perceptions of competence often underestimate the actual level of competence.
- Seeing each child as an individual is important: responses based on inflexible generalizations or stereotyped assumptions are not useful.
- Power relations are important to acknowledge and to try to work with as sensitively as possible.
- Adult priorities are often challenged by children's competence and involvement, and adults may seek to use the issue of competence as avoidance.

Guidance from research and practice sources

Table 4.3 offers a series of reflections on problematic issues regarding competence and links them to directions for developing a more effective relationship between children and adults. It draws on research and writing about practice in a variety of arenas and draws out directions.

The directions are informed by the new sociology of childhood in relation to competence.

Table 4.3 Competence and capability: issues and directions

Issue	Direction
Assessing children's experiences primarily from adult perceptions	Assessing child-based outcomes that include and prioritize children's, as well as adult's, perceptions
Using parents as proxies and treating children of all ages as having the same concerns	Ask children directly for their views in ways that are developmentally sensitive
Our knowledge of children's ability to understand and act on specialized areas such as medical information is incomplete	Better understanding of children's conceptualization of particular areas, such as health and illness, will help resolve some of the legal and ethical debates about whether children of different ages and intellectual abilities can give informed consent
Adults often withholding information from the perspective of 'protecting' the child	Respect research findings that evidence children's desire to be informed
Many information sources do not take account of the different needs of children in relation to different ages, or issues such as learning disability, or are directed at parents	Children's ability to participate competently in decision making and give informed consent can be improved by appropriate and specially developed information sources and appropriate ways of delivering material
Research into children's ideas about health and illness has been dominated by an overly rigid Piagetian perspective	Work using methods such as 'draw and write' or role play, has begun to demonstrate children's conceptualizations more aptly. These methods need to be used more extensively
Treat all children the same, as if their age was the only indicator of pre-conceived adult set standards of competencies	Respond to children whose experiences may facilitate the development of competencies beyond their chronological age. Better methods for assessing the competence of children of different intellectual abilities, including those who have learning disabilities

Activities

The following activities are designed to help reflect back on some of the key concerns over the chapter as a whole.

⇨

Activities—Cont'd

Chapter activity 1

A central idea is that 'Competence' is not a simple attribute that a child either possesses or does not possess: much will depend on the relationship and trust between those involved: children, parents and professionals.

How do you see this issue of trust and relationship present within the research in 'Examples of research: **children, divorce and separation**' and 'Examples of research: **power dynamics and believability**'?

Chapter activity 2

By using whatever information they have, children will continually try to make sense of their situations. An incomplete ability to understand does not justify a lack of discussion with a child who desires involvement in his or her care and decision making (Kriecbergs et al., 2004).

Review the research in 'Example of research: **decisions during hospitalization**'.

Do you think this research supports the assertion that an incomplete ability to understand doesn't justify discussion?

How do adults compromise or support the opportunity to help children 'try to make sense' of their situation within the reports of the research?

Chapter activity 3

Dixon-Woods, Young and Heney (1999) said:

> A key anxiety in creating partnerships with children is uncertainty about children's competence and how it can be assessed in different ages and abilities. Despite the suggestion that children should be assumed to be competent unless demonstrably incompetent, it is easy to assume that children are competent only if they make the decisions doctors want them to make. The children's rights movement might see this as paternalism, but it also reflects the fact that our knowledge of children's ability to understand and act on medical information is incomplete.

How do you see the relationship between the tensions described within this chapter viewing doctor's and children's competence in terms of paternalism or child rights?

Summary

This chapter has:

- looked at the ways adult attitudes to capability in relation to children and young people can result in a vicious circle of stereotyping and conforming to stereotypes of incompetence;

- examined ways in which an emerging agenda challenges ideas and practices rooted in seeing children as immature or incapable;
- looked at the relationship between research that offers insights into the ways of seeing children as capable and competent;
- reviewed research that examined ideas and practices in medical and hospital contexts regarding the child as an active agent in their use of services;
- reviewed research that engaged with children as capable critics of their school experiences;
- reviewed research that explores the idea of how practice can change to respond to children as capable and competent.

Further reading

Forrester, M. A. (2002) 'Appropriating cultural conceptions of childhood: participation in conversation', *Childhood*, 9, 255–76.

Research into everyday conversations and the ways in which children position themselves within interactions with parents, grandparents and other children.

Graham, M. (2007) 'Giving voice to black children: an analysis of social agency', *British Journal of Social Work*, 37, 1305–17.

Looks at the relationship between marginalization, black children and research concerning their lived experiences in social institutions. The paper looks at participatory approaches to involving black children in social care contexts.

Madge, N. (2006) *Children These Days*. Bristol: Policy Press, Chapter 4.

Draws on research into children's and adult's perceptions and experiences of notions of competency and capacity. The chapter looks at issues concerning decision making, physical and biological maturity, the law, age and the concept of 'growing up'.

Research details

Children, divorce and separation

Research by Mantle et al. (2006) looked at the issue of the 'age of the child' regarding welfare reports made in the context of divorce and separation by CAFCASS practitioners (Children and Family Court Advisory Service). These reports are made by practitioners working with the children. Those writing reports are obliged to establish the child's wishes and feelings. The involvement of children in mediation in such situations as well as parents and carers is an emerging area of practice. The research involved reviewing data of 1586 children who are the subject of welfare reports and in-depth interviews with twelve law practitioners. The children were spread across different ages: 25 per cent aged 4 or under, 42 per cent aged 5 to 9 and 32 per cent aged 10 and over. The researchers noted that within emerging practice, professionals 'make a number of assumptions about the child's competence based on chronological age' (2006, 499).

Decisions during hospitalization

Peer-reviewed journal. The research (2002) followed twenty-four children between 5 months to 18 years in a hospital looking at the degree of participation in decisions concerning their own care. Different levels of involvement were agreed and the researchers used these to evaluate 137 individual interactions between children, staff and families.

Power dynamics and believability

Peer-reviewed journal. The researchers (Duckett, et al., 2008) were approached by a Local Education Authority to help them understand 'children's sense of well-being in school'. This was linked to the UK National Healthy Schools programme introduced in 1999. The LEA had co-opted three local schools to become involved in a research project 'to explore how school demoted and promoted pupil well-being'. The research team framed their approach as 'to gain a rich contextualized understanding of pupils' psychosocial experience of school life and how this was implicated in well-being and explore future ways of working with the LEA to implement positive social change in those schools' (Duckett et al., 2008, 93).

Babies, Barbies and Blues: stereotyping and its challengers

Introduction and key questions

This chapter looks at adult attitudes towards children in terms of gender, and will approach this area of children's lives by looking at their imaged world. Contemporary society creates a separate set of images to accompany children in their lives: they find them in their environment from waking to sleep, and they inhabit their dream world. It is now so much a part of society that we assume it is normal – but this level and type of saturation is a remarkably recent phenomenon. The imagery is largely created, or influenced, by adult attitudes and interpretations of childhood, or adult-run national and international corporations. The chapter will draw on recent research to examine the processes, products and impact of attitudes towards children's gender.

- What are adult attitudes towards children's gender?
- Why do adults pink and blue children? Babies and beyond
- What is the impact of the ways adults try to gender children's worlds?
- How do children respond to their gendered world? How do they make their worlds in terms of gender and image?
- What are the implications of research on living and working with children?

What are adult attitudes towards children's gender?

Childhood is accompanied by a surround of made images and attitudes. An environment is created for children by adults in a number of ways. This consists of their physical space: material introduced into their lives through national and international media, as well as through educational materials and self- or peer-produced imagery. The environment includes the colours of their rooms, posters, lighting, toys and objects in the home, imagery directed at them in the street and at school. Their image environment includes material introduced through television, computers, advertising, books, music, magazines and comics. In addition, new media has created and enabled a set of images circulated by massive profit-seeking organizations and by peers through mobile phones, internet, Bebo or MySpace, and imagery produced by children themselves, or their immediate others. This last category is statistically small; the majority of children are mostly surrounded by images produced for them.

In terms of images produced for consumption during childhood, research has examined them in relation to the ways children are depicted as innocent or as sexualized, for example. It has looked at the presence of processes such as stereotyping in terms of gender, race or economic status – as discussed in Chapter 2. The images do not occur in a vacuum, they are delivered through particular media such as television or the web, which affect the meaning and impact of the images. They are received in a particular context – the lived situation of the child. This context includes factors such as the attitudes within the family home, or the child's community, towards aspects of the child's life such as gender roles, economic aspiration, the nature of love and care. Research such as that by Das Dasgupta (1998) has looked at the dynamics of factors such as ethnicity and immigration within this and how, for example, immigrant parents may attempt to ensure the transmission of their cultural values to the next generation. The contexts and the images have a relationship to each other in terms of their impact on any child.

This chapter draws on research that relates to a particular aspect of this image environment: gender. It is one that is crucial to children as they negotiate different parts of their lives. Here we will find microwaving Barbie to be a commonplace response within some groups of children, and adults providing pink nappy changers with princesses on for their female babies. As an arena of research it is one that is highly politicized and contested. Any act of research, or practice, with children takes place within a set of debates and positions that stand with, or against, ideas such as the nature and nurture debate, feminist positions that challenge inequality and right-wing politics that oppose ideas about equity and equality, for example.

Any attempt to examine attitudes towards children and gender must steer a way through these different agendas and powerful concerns. The approach of this chapter is to select and review ideas and research as a way of considering *how* to explore some key issues concerning adult and child attitudes towards children and gender.

Many of the pieces of recent research that this chapter looks at draw on ideas that gender is not something that is static and fixed. The following key

---

Key points: sex, gender and gender assessment

- Gender is seen as something that exists within the way we interact together rather than being something fixed by biology or society. The idea is that this is happening all the time, but that we tend not to notice it as, along with other areas examined in this book, we are often so inside the processes we do not have the perspective to see what is occurring.
- Sex, by contrast, is biologically based and is a 'determination made through the application of socially agreed upon biological criteria for classifying persons as females or males'.
- Gender is seen as an 'accomplishment', that is, something that occurs through interactions between people and that we use to organize social encounters.
- West and Zimmerman also argue that we do not always engage with gender in a way that lives up to general expectations and current definitions on how to look or behave – to 'live up to normative expectations'. They go on to say that to do this is 'to engage in behaviour at the risk of gender assessment' (1987, 136).

point summary draws on West and Zimmerman (1987), Fenstermaker and West (2002) and Deutsch (2007), whose work relates to this approach.

This way of seeing sex stresses that we agree on a difference based in biology – male and female, for example. This is then communicated, 'established and sustained' by identifying ourselves though behaviour or clothing, which are seen as 'displays that proclaim one's membership in one or the other category' (West and Zimmerman, 1987, 127). Gender is seen as something that we create around this difference: through behaviours towards each other, or interactions between us that are seen as expressions of masculinity or femininity. Crucial to this way of understanding gender is that these are *not fixed*, but are made by us, and these are changed and managed by individuals and groups (Fenstermaker and West, 2002).

In a sense, much of the research reviewed in this chapter involves trying to make such processes *visible*. The researchers also tend to emphasize in their approach and in their findings that if you see gender as something that is not fixed, but that people create through the ways they act and treat each other, then this makes it something that can be changed. This challenges ideas that the ways that males and females behave are set in stone, so it becomes something that can be seen, examined and then actively engaged with. Many of the researchers refer to West and Zimmerman's work in this area.

Deutsch (2007) has looked at how these ideas can form a useful direction for researchers. She argues that research should focus on how this approach can be used to foster needed change in order to challenge inequality. Looking at, for example:

- when and how social interactions become less gendered
- whether gendered interactions always underwrite inequality
- how institutions and individuals work together to produce change in areas that currently reinforce prejudice or inequality between people
- the idea of the way we interact as offering possibilities for change.

(Deutsch, 2007)

These concepts can be helpful when considering research and attitudes towards children. One notion, from these key points, is that part of the process of being involved in the way we see, and interact, with gender expectations is to stray from, or expand on, what is currently seen as the norm. Some adults and children challenge and explore, but others 'gender assess': they police or regulate what is seen as a norm. Bullying, for example, is an action taken at one extreme of such gender assessors, but comments, teasing and more subtle encouragement to conform are also part of the assessors' arsenal.

Some of the research in this chapter examines, for example, the ways in which gender identities of children are assessed and policed by their parents, or by other children if they stray from the established images and conduct of contemporary norms. Other research will look at the ways in which current norms of maleness and femaleness are seen as constraining for children, and as underwriting prejudice and unequal treatment. It looks at how such inequality is being challenged and broadened by child and adult attitudes, and by their ways of relating to each other.

Are children passive in the face of the influence of the imagery adults create around them? Do they challenge, contest and appropriate the influences? What images do children themselves create, and how do they relate to these processes? Emerging research, for example, seems to suggest that some children do not consume and passively adhere to adult-created and adult-initiated images of princesses and action men: the codes of stereotyped ideas fed to them. This chapter looks at these areas in terms of what they can tell us about attitudes towards children and the interaction between adult-supplied images and children's responses. As a way of highlighting issues and processes at work, particular ages and issues will be selected as illustrative examples.

Why do adults pink and blue children? Babies and beyond

Parents choose to create an environment for the early years of their child: rooms are painted, clothes are bought, toys are provided. These are not neutral. One way of looking at this environment is to see it as a way in which adults and children communicate and situate themselves in relation to gender, for example. Colour can be seen in this way as one area in which adults communicate or regulate their children's world: the choice they make of the colour of objects, lights, bedding, clothing, for example. In many countries a baby is born into a highly gendered environment. Few parents would create a pink room for a boy child to be cradled in from his first night. Why is this? Are girl babies born with a liking for pink, or boys with a need to be in a blue environment?

Example of research: both sexes prefer blue . . . but actually females prefer pink

In *Current Biology*, Hurlbert and Ling (2007) report on 208 adults' responses to 750 different pairs of colours from across the rainbow. They invited each participant to indicate which two shades they preferred. The participants were aged between 20 and 26 and were divided equally between men and women. Hurlbert and Ling based their research in 'the prevalence and longevity of the notion that little girls differ from boys in preferring pink'.

The actual finding was that both sexes rated blue as their colour of choice. However, the presentation of the findings in the media did not focus on this: rather the interest was that men tended toward 'purer blues' and the women for blues with 'pinkish undertones'. This was quickly turned by the media into 'At last, science discovers why blue is for boys but girls really do prefer pink' – one example of a headline by the UK's *The Times* newspaper's science editor (Henderson, 2007). The study did not examine the complex cultural processes at work within the making and communicating of such choices. It is interesting to look at how the research was interpreted in terms of the pinking and blueing of babies. The finding that both sexes choose blue is put into the background by the research conclusions and the media response. What is suggested in the researchers' reflections on their findings is that the liking for 'pinkish hues' could be because women 'in their roles as caregivers and empathisers' might need to notice subtle changes in skin colour or because females were thought to have done most of the fruit gathering from days when humans were 'on the savannah'. The article does not state whether savannah berries were blue, red or pink. The media tended to completely ignore the fact that blue was chosen by both sexes, and the fact that the researchers speculated, rather than stated, that the research indicated anything about innate liking for pink or blue, running with headlines about females being 'hardwired' to liking pink.

Another way of re-reading this, though, is to suggest that the research and its interpretation says much more about the current cultural desire to firmly segregate and regulate children in terms of gender. This is so entrenched in adults that even when both genders choose the same colour, the pinking and blueing process that we see at work in the adult treatment of babies runs through the interpretation of adult biologist researchers analysing their results. It even stretches to the need of the researchers to create imaginative and simplistic speculations about a fantasy prehistoric savannah life in order to force their findings to reinforce cultural stereotyping.

Reflections on the research
Activity 1

Reflecting on Hurlbert and Ling's research and the above commentary, how do you think parents are affected by the following in creating blue and pink environments for babies?

⇨

Area	Example
Societal pressure	Perceptions of other people
Their own perceptions of gender	Their own sense of what is appropriate for children
Marketing	The ways large corporations create targeted advertising
Economic factors	It might be more difficult to find affordable goods that are not pink or blue

Activity 2

In one of the key theoretical books on colour, archaeologist and ethnologist Varichon (2006) details the enormously complex cultural forces that operate in this area of our lives. He looks at the history of colours and the way they have featured in different cultures in different eras. Looked at in this perspective, blue, for example, has variously played the role in Roman life as the colour of mourning, and up to the fourteenth century in Europe it was associated with bad luck, until the cult of the Virgin Mary changed its associations.

Hence, wrapping a boy baby in blue within a culture where the association was mainly with mourning, might be parallel to current Westerners wrapping boy babies in funereal black at birth as the colour of choice. It is interesting to note that in the UK, for example, in the eighteenth century blue was considered a girls' colour and what we would now call pink, pale red, was considered a colour for boys, as red was considered to represent strength.

How do you relate this perspective to the findings and media response to the work of Hurlbert and Ling on blue and pink?

The powerful commercial enterprise, Disney, as we will see, have recently extended the most successful of their branding, the Princess range, to include nappy changing mats with pink princesses on them. Even in changing nappies, a number of parents, consciously or unconsciously, create a rigorously controlled environment where gender is segregated. Children are drawn into a set of images that corporations provide and parents supply into the world of their children, virtually as soon as they draw breath and open their eyes. Jones et al. (2007) have commented on the passivity of small children compared to older ones in relation to the world of images that adults create for them. They conclude that infants and most young children have 'limited input regarding the design of their environment and the specific items that are in their room. Whereas many older children and adolescents participate in the design of their bedrooms, for infants and children niche-building behavior is likely to be more passive than active' (2007, 15).

The imagery of the home bought by parents, and, as they age, influenced by children, is created by choices from materials produced by multinational organizations who have their own agendas. Large amounts of money are made from this, and clearly there is a very considerable global market for gendered goods with clearly differentiated blue and pink imagery.

What does this help us see in terms of adults, children and early years?

- Despite some claims that try to move in that direction, no research has effectively demonstrated that 'innate' needs of babies for blue or pink have any role to play in the choice to create such a world of imagery.
- Yet, as Disney profits indicate, many adults choose to rigidly 'pink' and 'blue' their babies' and children's worlds.
- One of the effects of this process is that children are born and grow within an environment that constantly feeds them with stereotyped images of what they could, or should, be like.
- Children's rooms, clothes, objects offer them a version of the world which adults want them to see.

Research findings suggest that adults project their desires for what childhood should be like, about what they wished their own childhood should have been like, into children's experiences. Some research has suggested that adults enforce the gender identity of their children as a way of reinforcing their *own* gender identity (Kane, 2006). Adult activity combines personal insights, intentions, nostalgia, psychological and emotional needs, as well as transmitting wider cultural beliefs or tensions about childhood and the relationship between adults and children, or models for relationships between people or models of community, economics and religious belief.

Some commentators and researchers (Fenstermaker and West, 2002; Messner, 2000) link these to the ideas of hegemony: the process by which a dominant culture maintains its position and dominance. This is not necessarily a deliberate process, but whether deliberate or not, it is the way one set of ideas, held by a powerful group, keeps the status quo of ideas and ways of living. Researchers have, for example, observed that parents place toys and images of vehicles, machines and sports equipment in boys' bedrooms, and dolls and flower imagery in girls' rooms. After reviewing a sample of rooms for children aged 6 and under, researchers found that none of the boys' rooms contained images and objects traditionally seen as feminine, such as dolls, and that girls' rooms contained none that were traditionally seen as masculine such as vehicles (Pomerlean et al., 1990; Rheingold and Cook, 1975). Rheingold and Cook concluded that such stark gender differences in young children's rooms were largely a result of parental selection.

What is the impact of the ways adults try to gender children's worlds?

Academics have paid attention to these adult activities and adults' supply of images by identifying trends or themes. Some are seen to pervade childhood as a whole across categories such as age difference between small children and teenagers, gender, race or economic status. Others are themes that are identified as occurring in images directed at particular age groups or to specific genders, or to the children of those in poor or rich households. The electronic screen, for example, plays a dominant part in children's lives. TV and computers are omnipresent. The UK's National Consumer Council research was with 557 children aged 9 to 13 and looked at the relationship between media exposure, and children's well-being. Their research revealed that children sit in front of screens before they go to school and when they come back from school. In some communities a third of families accompany mealtimes with TV programmes and even the computer (Nairn et al., 2007, 57).

There seems to be a divergence in parental regimes in UK households, with children from different backgrounds accessing radically different content and in different quantities. Children living in deprived areas are heavier users of both TV and computers than their affluent counterparts, and more of them visit chat rooms (Nairn et al., 2007, 23).

Some research that explored the role of access to gender-related imagery in new media, for example, connects to the way children and young people develop their concepts of their own and other's gender. Peter and Valkenburg's work in the Netherlands investigated 745 adolescents' exposure to what they described as an adult-created 'sexualised media environment' and their notions of women as 'sex objects' (2007). Ward and Friedman's (2006) study involving 244 adolescent of the same age group in the USA. Both concluded that adolescents' exposure to a sexualized media environment created and provided by adults is associated with developing stronger notions of women as sex objects.

The seemingly simple act of decorating a room, or providing access to media or giving playthings is intimately connected with factors of adult influence and intent. Attitudes towards childhood and children are deeply present within each item and each transaction.

Research has explored the ways in which parents and children interact with each other. The following example echoes some of the concerns identified so far – issues of pink and blue, gender stereotypes and the way parents respond to their children are examined through questionnaires and interviews concerning gender nonconformity.

Kane's (2006) research into USA parents' responses to gender nonconformity examines the ways attitudes are communicated and regulated by adults. She analysed parents' descriptions of their actions and responses to their children, in relation to gender. Children were aged between 3 and 5. The details of participants' backgrounds in the description of the research are from the researcher's text.

Example of research: children, parents and gender nonconformity

Kane's research discovered the following attitudes, drawing on common themes within the responses. The quotes are selected from her research, presented as illustrations of the key points:

Attitudes towards daughters

- Parents often 'celebrated' gender nonconformity on the part of their daughters by:
  - buying them toy cars and building toys
  - encouraging them in what they regarded as 'traditionally male occupations such as football and fishing' (2006, 156–7).
- No parents commented in a primarily negative way about daughters' perceived gender nonconformity.

Sample comments:

> She does a lot of things that a boy would do.
>
> *White, middle-class, heterosexual mother*

> We do (a lot) of stuff that's not stereotypically female.
>
> *White, upper-middle-class, lesbian mother*

⇨

> I never wanted a girl who was a little princess . . . I want her to take on more
> masculine characteristics.
>
> *White, upper-middle-class, heterosexual father*

Attitudes towards sons

In 'stark contrast' to the lack of negative responses for their daughters twenty-five of the thirty-one gave some positive responses in areas such as boys' domestic abilities or nurturing and empathy, but:

- twenty-three of the thiry-one parents of sons expressed some negative responses;
- six of these twenty-three offered only negative responses about perceived gender nonconformity in their sons;
- negative responses concerned areas such as wearing pink clothes or playing dress up in any kind of female clothing;
- parents expressed concerns about the following in their sons – excessive emotionality such as crying, or passivity;
- seven of the heterosexual fathers reported refusing their sons tea sets, nail polish or Barbies.

Sample comments:

> He asked about wearing girls clothes before and I just said no . . . He likes pink, and I try not to encourage him to like pink just because, you know, he's not a girl . . . There's not that many toys I wouldn't get him, except Barbie.
>
> *White, low income, heterosexual mother* (2006, 160)

> I would steer him away from a pink shirt as opposed to having him wear a blue shirt
>
> *Asian-American, middle-class, heterosexual father* (2006, 160)

> He's passive not aggressive . . . and I do worry about him being an easy target.
>
> *White, working-class, heterosexual mother* (2006, 162)

Sexual orientation

Sexual orientation came up as an issue. The findings showed a stark difference in attitudes towards girls and boys:

- No spontaneous connections between gender nonconformity and sexual orientation were made in comments about daughters, or in any of the comments by lesbian and gay parents.
- A fifth of heterosexual mothers and a third of heterosexual fathers responded negatively to the possibility of their son being, or being perceived as, gay (2006, 165). These comments included:

⇨

Example of research—Cont'd

> if a son was 'acting feminine' she would act to 'make sure he's not gay'
>
> *White, low income, heterosexual mother*

> fears that playing with toys meant for girls would shape their son's eventual sexual orientation, one commented that this would be an indicator of his 'failure as a dad'
>
> *White, upper-middle-class, heterosexual father*

The following gives one specific area in more detail. The researcher notes that heterosexual, lesbian and gay parents all displayed an awareness that 'their son's' behaviour was at risk of gender assessment, an awareness rarely noted with regard for daughters (2006, 165). Eleven of the seventeen heterosexual and lesbian mothers expressed fears that their sons might be treated negatively by adults and peers if they were not sufficiently masculine (2006, 167) in areas such as the colour of clothing.

Sample comments:

> [One worrying that her son had dressed in a pink princess costume:] I was worried they were going to think I was some kind of nut and next thing you know, send a social worker in . . . there are people out there who would think that's really wrong, and I was afraid.
>
> *White, upper-middle-class, heterosexual mother* (2006, 168)

> I feel held up to the world to make sure that his masculinity is in check or something.
>
> *White upper-middle-class, lesbian mother* (2006, 169)

The following broad conclusions were made from the research:

- Most parents made efforts to accomplish masculinity in their sons and either 'endorsed or felt accountable' to an ideal of masculinity defined by 'limited emotionality, activity rather than passivity, and rejection of material markers of femininity'.
- No similar pattern of well-defined normative negative expectations or accountability were present in interviews regarding daughters.
- Positive responses for daughters were made in relation to pursuits viewed as typically masculine.

Reflections on the research
Activity 1

The researcher comments that the research findings:

> may reflect the same devaluation of femininity evident in negative responses to gender nonconformity among sons.
>
> (2006, 172)

⇨

How do you see this comment relating to the different treatments and attitudes towards boys and girls in the findings?

Activity 2

In the conclusions to the enquiry the researcher comments that 'I began this project expecting that parents accept with little question ideologies that naturalize gender difference. Instead the results I have presented here demonstrate that parents are often consciously aware of gender as something that they must shape and construct, at least for their sons' (2006, 172).

How do you think this interpretation – of parents being actively involved in constructing and shaping their child's gender – can be used to see the findings offering an opportunity to broaden children's experiences of gender?

Activity 3

How do you see children's role in this process? What kinds of relationship might they have to the attitudes and responses of their parents described in this research?

Interview with Emily Kane about her research

Dr Emily Kane, Chair of Sociology, Bates College, Maine, USA

Phil Jones: **How do you see the role of research such as yours in relation to challenging attitudes towards children?**

Emily Kane: I hope that my findings in regard to parental feelings and actions in response to gender nonconformity would encourage readers to recognize the social construction of children's gender. It is easy to assume that children's gender–stereotypical interests, behaviours and attributes flow naturally from their biological sex, but as my findings indicate, children often stray from what gender stereotypes predict. When that happens, many parents intervene to discourage atypical gender performance. Even if their motivation is to protect their children from social stigma, as I note it often is (especially for heterosexual mothers and gay parents), when parents discourage their children's non-stereotypical gender performance, they are constraining their child's development and self-expression. Thus, at least some of what might appear to be naturally unfolding sex difference is, in fact, the result of parents constraining their children's development. It is important to recognize children as active agents in their own development, but also to recognize the instances in which adults curtail that agency, as the latter are important barriers to that agency.

Phil Jones: What did you learn about the process of researching from this experience?

Emily Kane: This research was part of the first qualitative interview study I conducted after having spent many years engaged in quantitative research drawing on large-scale public opinion data. I learned many things about the process of researching from the experience. As just one example, something I found striking when I began to analyse the interview transcripts was that I sometimes missed important opportunities to probe my interviewees' responses. When the topic of our interview conversation was comfortable for me, I probed effectively for detail, followed up on implications, etc. But when interviewees made implications that suggested an exchange I might find uncomfortable, such as implying a homophobic attitude with which I would disagree, I unconsciously backed off from probing fully. In retrospect, my best guess is that I did this in order to maintain a positive rapport with the interviewee, not wanting to encourage them to say something that would make it more difficult for me to feel genuinely positive towards them. This taught me the importance of listening back to interviews immediately and beginning to analyse patterns before conducting additional interviews, so that the researcher can correct any such tendencies. If I had realized I was doing this along the way, I would have been more careful to probe fully regardless of the topic/implication, as this would have resulted in richer, more nuanced, and more comprehensive interviews.

How do children respond to their gendered world? How do they make their worlds in terms of gender and image?

One of the key questions explored by academics and research is whether individual parents, families and children are passive in the face of such imagery and forces at work within society, or whether they have an individual voice. The way such ideas and images of femininity and masculinity are received or used, it can be argued, develop over time, and are subject to wide and diverse cultural influences. Here is a combination of diverse cultural processes, reflecting areas such as ethnicity and economic diversity. The next two pieces of research are included to explore aspects of this.

Example of research: children's bedroom culture

O'Donohoe and Bartholomew (2006) conducted research in Scotland with thirty-nine 10- to 12-year-olds, who were in either in their last year of primary school (P7) or their first year of secondary school (S1). One of the key aims was to gain insight into children's lives and to try to set the agenda for discussion from the child's point of view. Given the importance of bedroom culture to young people (Baker, 2004), they were asked to take some pictures of their bedroom. The resulting photographs were used to develop individual interviews.

The photographs within the research revealed a 'vast array of heroes and role models were evident in the children's bedrooms, in the form of posters, pictures, "shrines", and even hand-drawn sketches and artistic impressions'.

Within their findings the researchers comment on gender divisions in relation to the images the children have selected.

The values placed on the images by boys within the interviews were:

- to possess their heroes' sporting skills;
- being as 'good at golf' as Tiger Woods (quote from boy);
- 'brilliant at football' like David Beckham (quote from boy).

They contrast this with the girls who, within the interviews:

- talked about joining a pop band and becoming famous;
- emphasized how young stars could be 'good role models' and 'just normal people like we are';
- stressed the emotional and empathetic dimensions of identification. The research quotes one girl, for example, commenting on the appeal of images from *Home and Away*:
  o I just like the people that are in it, and the things that they do, and like if they've got problems and that, and they're trying to sort them out.

(O'Donohoe and Bartholomew, 2006, 10)

The research found that gender images, generally from media sources or branded goods within the bedrooms, were strictly audited by the children according to rigid definitions of male and female. The researchers noted that the boys were keen to distance themselves from 'feminine' activities, toys and ads, and from 'gay' brands and celebrities. They contrast this with the girls' important possessions, which emphasized emotional attachments and social (often romantic) links. In terms of images from marketing and advertising, researchers noted that 'the children enjoyed and elaborated upon ads which highlighted or enhanced their gender identity' (2006, 19).

⇨

Example of research—Cont'd

From these interviews the researchers conclude that

> Interactions with traditionally male and female possessions appeared to reflect a deeper need to demonstrate and even ritualize their expected gender roles, especially for the boys. For example, quite a few boys in this study recounted subjecting 'feminine' toys such as *My Little Pony* or *Barbie* to a gruesome demise.
>
> (2006, 11)

Reflections on the research
Activity 1

The research refers to images largely supplied by adults, from programmes made by adults or from brands and posters developed by adults for profit, and for consumption by children. The research concludes, though, that children are not just passive consumers of these images, and suggests that within this process children are expressing and negotiating their gender identities.

The authors reflect on their discoveries by suggesting that this is a way of the boys and girls developing their own sense of their sexual identity, the boys in relation to masculinity, the girls to femininity. This is connected by the authors to the ideas of 'othering' as discussed in Chapter 3.

How do you see these ideas of 'othering' in relation to research's reports of the children's responses to the images of heroes and heroines, of the gender divide and the ways in which the boys, especially, reject or are encouraged to reject, certain images or products as being too 'feminine'?

Activity 2

There are many theories and approaches to trying to understand the kinds of phenomena the researchers found in terms of gender and imagery in the children's bedrooms. One approach that is interesting to consider in looking at this research is Social Identity Theory. This concerns how people form social identities and looks at how people form themselves into groups.

Turner and Reynold's (2004) work looks at how people act either in terms of being an independent individual or in terms of being a member of a group such as 'boys' or 'girls'. Batahala in her research into people's perceptions and gender suggests that neither acting just as a member of a group, nor acting as an independent individual 'is likely to occur in a pure form in real life. People's behaviour is unlikely to be fully determined by their group membership or to be completely independent from it' (2008, 10). She says that experimental evidence suggests, 'that social behaviour is an expression of both individuality and individual-as-group-member' (2008, 10).

This suggests that individuals behave in different ways partly influenced by group membership, and partly as an individual distinct from group identity. How do you see the research's findings about children's relationship to images in their bedrooms in relation to Batahala's suggestion?

Active or passive?

Alanen's (2001) study of children's daily lives in a Finnish town analysed the relationships between children and adults in terms of children 'self-positioning' themselves as 'children'. This idea contrasts with the effects of children being seen or positioned in relation to adults. The focus of her work included children's own ways of looking at and conceiving of themselves in relation to the different ways they experience their daily lives. The notion behind this approach to research with children is that it enables the researcher to better understand the child's own perspective. Nairn et al. (2006) have offered a related critique of approaches to understanding the effect of images on children in areas of the media such as advertising. They have asserted the view that most academic, marketing and government approaches to researching its effects have been informed by adult concepts of development, and by adult ideas about images and the way they effect people, or how they are used. They have advocated and used a different way of discovering how children respond to images that can be useful in considering research into images of gender.

Key points: children and media images

Nairn et al. (2006) make the following key points in relation to understanding the nature and impact of media images or brands. It is important to attempt to:

- understand the brand world from the child's point of view;
- access the words, concepts and ways of valuing used by children themselves, as they encounter the world around them in response to the 'commercialized consumer world' with its images, products and pressures;
- see how the children themselves constructed meaning from objects and phenomena such as celebrity images or mass-produced products such as toys or accessories, rather than looking at how they interpret the adult world, or adult ideas about products and images;
- understand that the process of giving meaning to objects and phenomena is a complex social process, and that collective group responses and processes of discussion and debate are important.

This perspective, then, argues that images and the contexts have a dynamic relationship between each other and that the child's own perspective and ways of looking at what things mean are important. This concerns finding out the attitudes of the child towards themselves and their lives, those involved in the child's life and the things such as images and objects that they encounter. The next section looks at this in terms of children's own attitudes compared with adult-provided material and messages about gender.

Barbies and princesses

In 2000, Disney brought together its heroines, such as Cinderella, Mulan, Pocahontas, Sleeping Beauty and Snow White, together into a brand called 'Disney Princess' and saw their profits reportedly go from 300 million dollars in global sales to reach 1.3 billion dollars within three years. The brand extends to sales in India, Russia and China. It is interesting to see the language Disney representative, Franklin, uses in relation to this reach into the imaginations of girls:

> It's fascinating to us that girls in India, China, and Russia have the same play patterns in dressing up and playing out the Disney lifestyle and we'll continue to grow those emerging markets.
>
> (Franklin quoted by Wilensky, 2007, 2)

The following is not presented for its value as research, but to examine the language and frameworks that the adults presenting their research use. This powerful organization with its far-reaching influence on the world girls inhabit says this:

> Disney's research shows that girls don't just want to be a princess, they want to be a Disney princess. A Princess whose personality, dreams, favourites and friends she knows from the stories she loves. And moms embrace the brand because in a time when little girls are maturing at a much faster pace, Disney Princess merchandise lets little girls be little girls longer. The stories behind the Disney princesses empower girls with virtues.
>
> (PR Newswire, 31 March 2004)

The princesses were initially aimed at 2- to 6-year-old girls, with images being present in many aspects of girl's lives from backpacks to shoes as well as video and print media. Later merchandizing targeted cribs and nappy changing mats.

As we have seen, children are surrounded by such images of gender in different ways. From the walls of the room they fall asleep and wake in, to the video games and television, to each other and the clothes they dress in and the ways they are encouraged to judge what a female and male body should look like or behave like, and in response to their own and each other's bodies. Classic analysis suggests that the images adults offer of female behaviour through dolls and advertising are that they should be thin, not eat and look at themselves and each other as objects. Of males it is that they should use guns, be violent and kill things.

What is the impact of this polemic that adult society creates and that children adopt or react to as they get older? Are they passive in the face of the Barbie images of thinness that surround them and that they surround themselves with, or as they engage with images of male violence that pass before them?

The idea that children consume and respond passively and uncritically to images, toys and ideas of gender is challenged by recent research that has investigated children's negotiating their own meanings and expressing their differences, with an emphasis on discovering the children's perspective and experience.

Example of research: Barbie torture

> C: I don't buy Barbies anymore. They're all dead . . .
> S: I torture mine.
> C: I hung them at Halloween. All their hair's cut as well. They're all GI Janes.
>
> *Girls, P7, private* (O'Donohoe and Bartholomew, 2006, 9)

Research by Nairn et al. (2006) examined the ways children interacted and used media and commercial products in their lives. Rather than being identified by adults, the researchers asked groups of children in a number of different junior schools in different socio-economic areas to create the focus for the research. They used devices such as the children brainstorming a list of 'the things kids in your class are into at the moment'. Other data involved exploring the children's ways of classifying them, the terminology they used to respond to different images, objects and activities. Hence the classifications most frequently used within the research were:

- quality
- cool
- radical
- minging
- pants
- rubbish.

The children drew on their experiences of TV programmes, celebrities, pop stars, styles, adverts, hairstyles, jewellery and magazines. Transcriptions of the children's taped discussions and the data collected through the brainstorming were analysed. The researchers note that this process of negotiation has not been reported or looked at in other research (2006, 12).

The researchers made no suggestions for the objects or brands for discussion, letting those arise from the children themselves. The analysis looked at areas such as:

- brands and media influences which were mentioned most consistently across groups and
- which generated excitement, interest and debate, that is, those which form social currency for these junior school children (Nairn et al. 2006).

The following focuses on the findings of the research in relation to Barbie.

The researchers note that although some of the girls did play with Barbies, there was a complicit agreement that it was not cool to admit to enjoying it, or that it was a last resort. However, they note that 'the meaning of "Barbie" went beyond an expressed antipathy. Actual physical violence and torture towards the doll was repeatedly reported, quite gleefully, across age, school and gender' (2006, 31).

Group Year 3 mixed:

Interviewer: What about Barbie?
All children: (loud and in unison) Boo!

⇨

Boy 1:	The one thing I like about Barbie is that they're quite good at destroying. My sister had one a very, very long time ago and I did like putting soap over them and burning them and breaking them.
Boy 2:	(with actions) You grab their hair and pull their heads off.
Girl:	My sister cut all of her hair off cause I used to have them and she cut off its hair and it was bald.

Group Year 6 girls:

Girl 1:	I still have loads of them so I can torture them.
Girl 2:	Me too.
Girl 3	I dye their hair.
Girl 1:	So I think I'll torture them and pull their heads off. Coz they are not particularly cool unless . . .
Interviewer:	They're not particularly cool unless you what?
Girl 1:	Torture them.

Group Year 3 mixed:

Girl 1:	Our friend does that with Barbies.
Girl 2:	Yeah, she microwaves them.
Girl 1:	Did she parachute one out of the house?
Girl 2:	Yeah, she parachuted one out of the house and it landed in the neighbour's garden.

The researchers explored the reasons behind the hatred and violence. The children's comments included:

- 'Barbie is hated because she is babyish.'
- 'Outgrown her.'

The researchers commented: 'Whilst for an adult the delight the child felt in breaking, mutilating and torturing their dolls is deeply disturbing, from the child's point of view they were simply being imaginative in disposing of an excessive commodity in the same way as one might crush cans for recycling.'

Year 3:

Interviewer:	What kind of people like Barbie?
Girl 1:	Babies.
Girl 2:	Sissies.
Girl 3:	Girls, um, not babies, but really girly girls.

Year 6, private school, mixed group:

Girl:	She's like Action man really, although she's a Barbie, and they just make programmes and adverts and movies and it's just so, a waste of their money, I think.

⇨

Example of research—Cont'd

Reflections on the research

Activity 1

One of the outcomes was that the researchers noticed how much there was rarely clear agreement as to what was 'quality' and what was 'minging'. Instead they discovered that the groups were often volatile, with different meanings and values being made and discussed.

How do you see the relationship between these findings and the following key points by Nairn et al. (2006) about discovering children's responses to media influences?

- The words, concepts and ways of valuing used by children themselves.
- To see how the children themselves constructed meaning from objects and phenomena.
- The complex social process and collective group responses and processes give meaning to objects and phenomena.

Activity 2

The research findings in 'Research example: children's bedroom culture' talks about similar findings regarding boys subjecting 'feminine' toys such as Barbie to 'a gruesome demise' and sees this as the demonstrating and ritualizing 'their expected gender roles' (2006, 11). The research by Nairn et al. (2006) reports both girls and boys 'breaking, mutilating and torturing' Barbies.

How much do you see the girls' responses to Barbie in relation to:

- the idea that they are negotiating their own meanings about gender rather than accepting adult-prescribed ideas about stereotyping?
- the notion that they are responding to the Barbies as not cool and not age-appropriate rather than anything concerning gender?
- a wider cultural attitude that reflects fear, hatred and the devaluing of the feminine?

Here, then, a more complex picture is revealed. The world of images does not exist on its own. It is not the only way the child's version of their own and others' gender is formed.

Research such as that summarized above is beginning to show that, importantly, a tension or relationship is set up between the images children encounter and the actual immediate environment and context they see them in.

In addition, it sees children as active in their own lives regarding gender, making their own meanings and practices. This sees children not as passive receptors of adult-created processes, products and gendered ways of reacting and relating, but as lively agents. This means that images of male and female toys, cartoons, boys, girls, women and men in the media are subject to discussion and active response, with people displaying different attitudes towards them. So, children react and make sense of these images within the ways they and others encounter them.

What are the implications of research on living and working with children?

Research shows a varied picture of adults' attitudes to stereotyping children, their impact regarding the lives of children and of children's responses. The following offers a snapshot of other research relating to some of the debates and issues raised within the in-depth examination of the research examined so far.

In their research into stereotyping and gender-stereotypic toys working with seventy-seven children, Serbin et al. comment, in line with much other research:

- that the socialization pressures on boys to act in accordance with stereotypes are much stronger than on girls;
- these come from many different sources such as parents, teachers and peers;
- they comment on the 'prescriptive nature of stereotypes . . . accordingly children are motivated to act in accordance with stereotypes' (2001, 7–8).

However, the presence of stereotypes does not mean that they are static, or that different communities or individuals respond to their presence in different ways.

Martin, for example, in her research into childcare advisors and gender-neutral child-rearing reflects the complex, changing and varied picture of contemporary child-rearing practices in the USA:

- some advisors give their seal of approval to 'gender-neutral parenting' even if 'they are unconvinced it will work';
- 'most advisors approve of behaviours that were nearly taboo 50 years ago – preschool boys playing with dolls, girls and boys playing together, girls playing sports and the like' (2005, 475).

However, she notes a theme that has run through much of the research in this chapter: there is an adult anxiety about boys and girls thinking 'of themselves as similar' as this connects to concerns about 'advocating' homosexuality.

From this she comments:

- this stigmatization needs to be addressed;
- there are few institutions, including feminist, lesbian, gay, bisexual or transgender ones that offer suggestions on 'how to raise people to be gay';
- the reasons why parental attitudes mean that they try to ensure heterosexuality in their children needs to be addressed;
- how parents respond to signs of homosexuality in children are important political and intellectual questions (2005, 475).

Kane sees the research findings in 'Research example: children, parents and gender nonconformity' as identifying some of the ways in which stereotyping within adult attitudes and practices hinder children. The ways parents set and maintain boundaries for their sons, for example, is interpreted by her as 'a crucial obstacle limiting boys' options' by:

- separating boys from girls;
- devaluing activities marked as feminine for both boys and girls;
- bolstering gender inequality and heteronormativity (2006, 173).

These findings are taken forward by Kane into implications regarding positive action in relation to such constraints:

- Evidence of conscious effort by adults, has implications for reducing gender constraints on children.
- Acknowledgement that parents are sometimes 'consciously crafting' their children's gender suggests that they could be encouraged to shift their efforts in less constraining directions (2006, 173).
- Parents' openness in their attitudes to domestic skills, nurturance and empathy in their sons 'likely represents social change'. If masculinity is historically variable in its content, then some broadening of that content may be occurring.
- The observation that gender boundaries are enforced could serve to motivate broadening normative conceptions of masculinity, and challenge the devaluing of femininity, to broaden and value ways of children behaving, seeing themselves and seeing and relating to others.

Renold (2002) has looked at sexual harassment and schooling, drawing on data from the ways in which gendered attitudes can result and express themselves in sexual harassment and bullying based on gender and homophobic bullying in schools.

The ways the children respond to masculinity and femininity is seen by her research to be linked to the ways 'heterosexism, homophobia and heterosexual harassment are experienced and carried out by both boys and girls as they negotiate and maintain gender and sexual hierarchies and hegemonies' (2002, 417):

- Children are active in the formation of their gender and sexual identities.
- Sexuality and specifically heterosexuality is 'part and parcel' of their gender identity constructions.
- Young children experience different forms of sexual harassment.
- Homophobia, heterosexism and heterosexual harassment provide ways of 'resecuring gender dichotomies' or splits, creating and maintaining masculinity as dominant and pacifying female, or gay, gender and sexualities, and that these are policed by some children (2002, 429).

These are taken by her into implications for adults and children:

- The need to include sexuality as an equal opportunity issue.
- The need to look at practices for working with sexual- and gender-based bullying in schools.
- The creation of a curriculum and policy framework that is sensitive 'to children's own sexual cultures' to engage with the 'more damaging and oppressive side to children's developing sexual and gender identities and peer relationships' (2002, 429).

This is seen by her to work towards changing the negative impact of gendering, prejudice against women and femininity, stereotyping and fear of difference.

Activities

The following activities are designed to help reflect back on some of the key concerns over the chapter as a whole.

Chapter activity 1

In the 'Key points: *sex, gender and gender assessment*', the idea was put forward that:

> Gender is seen as an 'accomplishment': that is, something that occurs through interactions between people and that we use to organize social encounters.

⇨

Activities—Cont'd

How do you see this in relationship to the research reported in 'Example of Research: **children, parents and gender nonconformity**' and 'Example of Research: **children's bedroom culture'**.

Pay particular attention to the way adults and children relate to each other in terms of their interactions regarding

- the power relationship between adults and children;
- the parallels and differences between the experiences of boys and girls within the interactions about their gender.

Chapter activity 2

In the summary of research findings (page 100), Kane is quoted as saying that one of the implications of her research is that 'the devaluing of femininity' could be challenged and that her work opens up possibilities, 'to broaden and value ways of children behaving, seeing themselves and seeing and relating to others'.

In 'Key points: *sex, gender and gender assessment*', Deutsch emphasizes the ways in which research can help combat attitudes that reproduce inequality. How do you think that the research contained within this chapter can connect to her proposals for research that helps discover how institutions and individuals work together to produce change in areas that currently reinforce prejudice or inequality between people?

Chapter activity 3

In the summary of research (page 99), Serbin et al. (2001) were reported as commenting that the socialization pressures on boys to act in accordance with stereotypes are much stronger than on girls.

Examining the research reported in this chapter, do you agree with this, or do you think the pressures are just different, rather than greater or lesser, between boys and girls?

Summary

This chapter has:

- looked at the ways adult attitudes to stereotyping and gender in relation to children and young people can result in pressure to conform;
- examined ways in which a child rights' agenda challenges ideas and practices rooted in seeing boys and girls within restricting gender stereotypes;
- looked at the relationship between research that offers insights into the way gender is constructed, and how this offers insights into the ways adults and children interact;

- reviewed research that examined ideas and practices concerning 'gender assessment' and both the ways in which the policing and regulation of gender occur;
- reviewed research that examined ideas and practices that looked at how stereotyping can be challenged;
- reviewed research that explores the idea of children as active agents in relation to attitudes that stereotype them.

Further reading

Buckingham, D. (2004) 'New media, new childhoods? Children's changing cultural environment in the age of digital technology', in Kehily, M. J. (ed.) *An Introduction to Childhood Studies*. Maidenhead: Open University Press.

A review of the extent and nature of the impact of new media on children, looking at issues around commerce and research that reflects the concept of children as sophisticated, discriminating users of media.

Nairn, A. and Griffin, C. (2006) 'The Simpsons are cool but Barbie's a minger: the role of brands in the everyday lives of junior school children'. Report, University of Bath.

A review of literature concerning children's exposure to commercially sponsored media in recent years in both Europe and the USA. Research that challenges developmental approaches to understanding such phenomena and looks at alternative theories and approaches to understanding children's interaction with phenomena such as brands.

Das Dasgupta, S. (1998) 'Gender roles and cultural continuity in the Asian Indian immigrant community in the US', *Sex Roles: A Journal of Research*, June, 1–9.

Research with Asian Indian parents and children in the USA exploring dynamics around gender, ethnicity and immigration, including concepts of cultural erasure and issues of parental attitudes towards 'Americanized' children.

Research details

Both sexes prefer blue . . . but actually females prefer pink

Peer-reviewed journal. The response of 208 adults to 750 different pairs of colours across the rainbow. Researchers invited each participant to indicate which two shades they preferred. The participants were aged between 20 and 26, white British and Chinese, equally divided between men and women.

Hurlbert, A. and Ling, Y. (2007) 'Biological components of sex differences in colour preference', *Current Biology*, 17, 16, R623.

Children, parents and gender nonconformity

Peer-reviewed journal. Questionnaires and interviews with forty-two US parents, mothers and fathers, four being in a married pairs, of children who each had at least one child aged 3 to 5. They were aged 23 to 49 years, including single- and two-parent families and were from a variety of backgrounds and class, racial and ethnic groups including white, Asian American and African American and heterosexual and lesbian and gay parents. The descriptions of background are from the researchers' descriptions.

Kane, E. (2006) '"No way my boys are going to be like that!" Parents' responses to children's gender nonconformity', *Gender and Society*, 20, 149–76.

Children's bedroom culture

Peer-reviewed journal. Research undertaken in Scotland with thirty-nine 10- to 12-year-olds, who were in either their last year of primary school (P7) or their first year of secondary school (S1).

O'Donohoe, S. and Bartholomew, A. (2006) 'The business of becoming: children, consumption and advertising in transition, child and teen consumption 2006'. Paper no. 37. Online: www.cbs.dk/content/download/41857/616432/file/

Barbie torture

Report, University of Bath. Seventy-two children from mixed UK junior schools in a small city in England: one private in the national top 5 per cent for academic achievement; one state below the national average for academic achievement. This selection was made in an attempt to cover a range of socio-economic backgrounds. Half the children were age 7/8 (Year 3) and half 10/11 (Year 6). In each school a third of the groups were girls only, a third boys only and a third mixed gender. Thus, in total, twelve discussions with six children were held in a quiet room in each school.

Nairn, A. and Griffin, C. (2006) 'The Simpsons are cool, but Barbie's a minger: the role of brands in the everyday lives of junior school children'. Report, University of Bath.

Fear for Children and Fear of Children: protection and projection

6

Introduction and key questions

This chapter will examine adult fear in relation to children. It will focus on two key areas of contemporary attitudes. The first looks at what research reveals about attitudes that surround and fuel fear for children's safety and security. The second will examine research that concerns phenomena relating to adults' fears of children.

Research can play a role in helping to see the ways adults project their own preoccupations onto children: it can help expose cultural anxieties at work within current 'fears' for children, and of children. Do adults build stereotypes, for example, and then use children and young people to *feed* their fears? If this is the case, why should this be? The chapter will look at ways research can help us understand the implications of these attitudes in relation to children's lives and those who live and work with them.

- What are adult attitudes concerning fear for, and fear of children?
- How do adult ideas and practices concerning our fear for children affect children's lives?
- How do adult ideas and practices concerning our fear of children affect children's lives?
- How can attitudes be challenged and changed?

What are adult attitudes concerning fear for, and fear of children?

Adult attitudes towards children contain powerful feelings, urges and needs. These exist in adults as individuals and are also experienced and expressed in large group contexts.

For individual adults these attitudes exist in our thoughts, feelings and dreams, and in the way we relate to children in our immediate lives. Examples of this concern how adults relate to their own children in families, to children they work with or those they meet in the street, and their feelings about their own childhood. These might be reflected in our ways of participating in the rearing of children, as parents or workers. They concern feelings that are created in us by the ways children in contemporary life are seen. Examples of this might be the way we are aroused by ideas and responses to feelings of care and need when encountering a baby, or by anxiety or fear when encountering a group of youths on a street at night. Research, which this chapter will refer to, shows that these attitudes are not constant. In particular, the attitudes at the focus of this chapter – fears for, and of, children – have seen recent, remarkable shifts.

The ways these shifts in attitude concerning adult fears combine with other factors to affect children's lives are complex. They have been analysed in relation to different arenas, such as their effect on state intervention in relation to children at risk, for example. In that sphere recent changes have occurred in attitude and policy which have had an important impact on the nature of adult intervention. Walker, for example, notes in the UK a 'shift from narrow "protection" following principles . . . of minimal state intervention, towards a broader approach to promoting children's welfare' (2008, 141). He connects this to changes in adult attitudes as expressed through policy: 'a change from the view of state intervention as being something to be wary about to it being welcome, if it is supportive' (2008, 141). This chapter does not seek to look at all areas surrounding such shifts and changes in social attitudes and their impact on the lives of children and young people. It will focus on some significant pieces of research that will allow us to explore the dynamics between adult attitudes concerning fear and the kinds of effects the attitudes have. This will involve research that examines the ways adults and children interact: whether this be in the arena of the large-scale policies adults create, or the smaller, individual, daily ways we interact with children in the street when they seem to be in danger or to be dangerous.

As noted earlier in this book, these individual attitudes are a combination of many things: our rational decision-making capacities, and our unconscious and repressed emotions and ideas. They reflect attitudes surrounding us from close others such as immediate family and community, as well as those from a wider perspective such as the media. They are a mixture of areas we are aware of, but importantly and profoundly, things we are not so aware of and yet which deeply and powerfully influence our attitudes and the actions they result in concerning children.

One significant context for these attitudes concerning fear involves the way adults as groups create phenomena and experiences for ourselves in relation to children and young people. I deliberately phrase it in this way as it emphasizes decision and agency. Often when engaged in large groups it can be felt as if things that happen are 'normal' or a 'given', rather than something which is made and created by adults in interaction with each other. Examples of this might be the way the media and very large groups of adults create phenomena such as panics or obsessions. Here powerful cultural, or large-group, dynamics and commercial interests combine to create phenomena. These include media panics about 'youth crime' or an obsession with a particular lost child, as we will examine later.

Another example is in the ways in which attitudes and large-group thinking and feeling combine to create national or local government policies, laws, procedures and ways of treating children. Adults often tell themselves that these are done within the sphere of rational decision making and negotiation. Such processes as media coverage of an issue, or the creation of a policy made through large groups in a series of meetings, proposals and decisions are made to seem as if they are purely or primarily the product of a certain kind of logical thinking and rationalizing. However, there are parallels with the earlier commentary on the different components of individual attitude and their impact on actions. With large group, community and national attitude, these, too, are often a combination of rational thought and powerful phenomena of which we are much less conscious and aware. They are often informed by cultural attitudes that we are not alert to, because we are so deeply enmeshed in the culture we live in and cannot easily see them. Another component of this aspect of the way adult attitudes affect children is the ways in which large groups can act irrationally, reflecting deeply seated, but often unconscious, phenomena. To be protective of children *and* to be frightened of children can seem to be so far apart that they appear unrelated. Looked at in this way, however, two seemingly opposite issues, at the forefront of our attitudes towards children, can become connected. Both combine individual and large-group processes linked to adult fear and children. This chapter will explore each separately, as well as the relationship between the two.

How do adult ideas and practices concerning our fear for children affect children's lives?

Recent research indicates that attitudes towards children in a variety of areas relating to fear and anxiety are volatile and have undergone, and continue to undergo, shifts. Awareness of, and research into, the extent of areas such as child maltreatment, abuse and neglect are problematic in locating and defining the exact extent of adult violence and abuse experienced by children. Statistical information gives some indication of the extent of children's abusive treatment at the hands of adults. In 2004, for example, data collected from US Child Protective Services determined that approximately 900,000 children in the United States were 'victims of child maltreatment and about 1,500 children died because of abuse or neglect' (Children's Bureau, 2006). A review of these figures says that 'these numbers likely underestimate the number of children affected by maltreatment due to underreporting and focus on a single data source' (Children's Bureau, 2008, 3). Figures for the UK in the same year, based on the Child Protection Register report a total of 26,300, including categories for physical, sexual and emotional abuse and neglect. Again the National Society for the Prevention of Cruelty to Children notes that these figures are not to be taken as representing the level of abuse as they record only those for whom there is a need for a child protection plan because of their being at continued risk of significant harm (NSPCC, www.nspcc.org.uk/Inform/resources-forprofessionals/Statistics/ChildProtectionRegisterStatistics/childprotect ionregisterstatistics_wda48723.html). Gardner (2008) concludes that research indicates that neglect and emotional abuse, broadly defined, are 'fairly common', drawing on research by Cawson et al. (2000) to conclude as an under estimation that 6 per cent of all young adults recall inadequate care and 18 per cent report humiliation or attacks on their self-esteem in childhood.

In the UK, data collected by the NSPCC concluded in 2007 that there had been significant increases in awareness of the prevention of cruelty to children as an important 'cause'. The research says 'currently 50% of adults cite protecting children from cruelty as the most important cause in society. This figure has risen from 16% in February 1999 to 50% in March 2007' (NSPCC, Key statistics, NSPCC inform www.nspcc.org.uk/inform/resourcesforprofessionals/ Statistics). Research conducted jointly by the NSPCC and the University of East Anglia commented on the public debate that, 'Cases of neglect are frequently reported in the press' but that 'the public response is ambivalent. The public seems to be concerned about emotional harm and neglect – but unsure that they warrant state intervention. There is concern for children but also for parents under stress in a risk averse culture' (Gardner, 2008, 20). Walker comments on this in relation to attitudes within society that relate to Gardner's comments, saying that, 'the attitude towards children . . . is that they are effectively the private property of parents' (2008, 140). The underlying ambivalent attitude towards children and childhood is summarized by him as a 'mixed message' that reflects and causes confusion which allows children to be harmed: 'child rearing is the responsibility of us all, but people other than parents can only exercise this responsibility without parental consent if the children are in danger' (2008, 141–2). Gardner's review of research in this area illustrates this ambivalence. She reports examples where teachers noted and reported signs of neglect in children: 'some of the children came to school hungry and brought no food with them. Others were unkempt and uncared for – with dirty, unlaundered clothes' (2008, 25). However, the problem identified was that in these cases they 'did not reach the social care threshold criteria for engagement. Children were left with or returned to carers with no further action' (2008, 25). She concludes that this attitude causes lack of clarity on what constitutes neglect and that this ambivalence is likely to contribute to an unacceptably high threshold for intervention, and, crucially, to 'uncertainty and delays' in preventative action (2008, 28), leading to children suffering repeated, unresolved neglect or other forms of maltreatment. Adult attitudes here contain, on the one side, loud public outcry and outrage, a rhetoric of anxiety with actions that prohibit children's freedom in aspects of their lives, alongside, on the other, an ambivalence over actual intervention when harm is occurring.

Why is there such volatility, such ambivalence as commented on by Walker (2008) and in Gardner's (2008) reflections on her research? What fuels adult attitudes in such areas?

Two examples that are at the core of this issue will be focused on as a way of exploring aspects of these adult attitudes and their impact on children. One concerns the ways in which, in our everyday lives, adults relate to the children in a family context. This looks at the dynamics within individual and large-group attitudes that have produced a significant shift in a relatively short period of time. This shift reflects a palpable concern experienced on one level by parents or guardians directly with their own children, and at another level by larger groups such as schools or government policy makers. It is that, outside of the family home, all children are not safe. This risk is from adult-perceived physical injury, molestation, sexual exploitation or emotional harm.

The other concerns the growing realization that adults who are in positions of care have been harming children, and that the cultural units and structures in existence, such as the family or services such as state or voluntary sector care homes, had become the opposite of what they were intended for. Instead of spaces and relationships for nurturing, loving and protecting children, they had become efficient traps to hold and silence children whilst they were harmed, abused and killed: a significant proportion by their fathers, male family members or by people known to children but not related to them (Cawson et al., 2000). This rapidly changing construction of childhood has been linked to the emergence of what Thorne rightly calls 'startling statistics' and of the previously hidden violence: 'the media, buttressed by social science findings, have given visibility to the problem of adult physical abuse of children, and, in recent years (due in part to the efforts of the contemporary women's movement) to the prevalence of adult sexual abuse of children' (1987, 90). Leonard (2007), in her work with teenagers on their perceptions of 'risky environments', describes this shift. From the private sphere of the family home being seen as a 'safe haven that children move outwards and explore the wider world' has 'in recent years' been increasingly questioned, as 'for some the home is one of the most common sites for the sexual abuse of children' (Leonard, 2007, 435) and its position changed (James et al., 1998).

The nature of danger and threat can be seen as a relationship between areas such as any actual danger to a child, or children, and the ways in which we frame, see and create the danger. In some areas such as child protection, the awareness of dangers to children has had positive effects on children's lives. Examining how adult concerns take shape, and the actions that are devised as responses to these concerns, can tell us about our attitudes and 'fear' in ways that serve children less well. It can help us identify how these have negative effects on children's lives in a variety of areas – such as health or play. Research findings, for example, indicate that in a number of societies children are engaging less in outdoor play, and that this can have negative effects on health, on the development of social skills and on their experience of living in a community (Department for Children, Schools and Families, 2008; Jarvis et al, 2008; Sutton-Smith, 2005). Boyland (2007) has identified a number of interconnecting factors that has created this reduction – such as adult intolerance of children playing in the street and local authority indifference to the creation of adequate play spaces. Focus group work also revealed issues connected to adults' fears for, and of children, and the kinds of recent shifts in attitude referred to earlier. Adults working in small focus groups were asked to produce two images: one representing play 'today', and one which represented play when the adults themselves were children. The research findings report a stark contrast. The images representing the adults' own experiences were of 'safety, green spaces, happiness, adventure' and those of contemporary play were on the whole 'negative' and were described as 'a lack of facilities, sterile, man-made facilities, fear, danger, idleness, yob behaviour . . . restrictions, being watched and violence' (Boyland, 2007, 13). Across all the focus groups the findings are described as highly consistent. The three greatest identified fears were 'stranger danger', anti-social violence and traffic. These were identified as reasons why parents would not allow children to play unsupervised. Moderators are described as pushing the adult participants about whether stranger danger was seen as a genuine growing threat, or a reaction to media coverage. Half felt that the threat had always been there but it was better known about now, with the rest feeling that the 'problem' has recently increased. Comments were also that whether the threat was real or only perceived, the restriction was the same. The research also showed that adults' fear for the safety for children was accompanied by a perception that adolescents were fearful. Adults commented on youth violence and that their perception was that parks were spaces that adolescents could 'hide' in, and it made them 'threatening areas' (2007, 23). The report cites one comment as representative: 'It's not only sex offenders: there's even kids as young as nine carrying knives' (2007, 24), and another 'I want my children to be walking home by themselves, I want them to be streetwise but now . . . you think it's not worth my child dying' (2007, 24). The research analysis concludes that a vicious circle is being created that will lead to a 'hardening' of parents and children's 'insularity'

(2007, 39). There are a number of complex factors within this analysis. However, for the purpose of this chapter, it highlights questions which analysis of other research will examine in more depth. These concern looking at how adult anxieties and perceptions shape children's lives, how the inter-relationship of adults' fears for children, and fear of children, fuels the way adults treat children, and whether such anxieties are rooted in reality. In exploring these questions the goal is to look at how to check which adult attitudes help, and which harm children, in order to examine how, where appropriate, they can be challenged in order to improve children's lives.

The following is interesting as an example of examining an emerging adult fear: the 'internet'. The review undertaken by Byron and her team in the UK summarizes evidence gathered from a number of research initiatives. It is interesting in the way it brings together:

- concepts of the reduction or absence of social norms, behaviour and control;
- perceptions of threatening external forces impinging on the 'safe' family;
- challenges to traditional family–child relations and notions of gate keeping;
- ideas of maturity and vulnerability.

Example of research: internet risk and the Byron review (2008)

The Byron review argues that evidence from child development and brain development literature indicates that 'age-related factors and understanding the ways in which children learn can provide a very useful guide to identifying and managing potential risks to children when using the internet or playing video games. This is particularly because of the development of a key part of the brain throughout childhood – the frontal cortex, which mediates their experiences and behaviour' (2008, 4). This is seen by the report authors to help navigate an approach to help guide adults as 'decreasing supervision and monitoring occurs with age as we judge our children to be increasing in their competence to identify and manage risks' (2008, 4).

They say that their data reveals risks to children and young people:

- increased 'exposure' to sexually inappropriate content;
- 'stranger danger';
- cyberbullying;
- access to 'inappropriate content from sites which may promote harmful behaviours';
- commercial content (2008, 4).

⇨

Internet risks can reflect offline issues such as bullying, but the problems are seen as 'qualitatively different and sometimes have the potential to be more damaging'. This is linked to the nature of the internet's 'anonymity, ubiquity and communication potential' (2008, 5).

They argue that research is beginning to reveal that:

> people act differently on the internet and can alter their moral code, in part because of the lack of gate-keepers and the absence in some cases of visual cues from others that we all use to moderate our interactions with each other.
>
> (Byron, 2008, 5)

From this they argue that this is:

> potentially more complex for children and young people who are still trying to establish the social rules of the offline world and lack the critical evaluation skills to either be able to interpret incoming information or make appropriate judgements about how to behave online.
>
> (2008, 5)

The report comments that:

> There is a generational digital divide between parents and children which means that many parents do not feel empowered to manage risks in the digital world in the same way that they do in the 'real' world.
>
> (2008, 3)

Reflections on the research
Activity 1

It is interesting to see what is foregrounded as a danger, and what is seen as less 'threatening'. So, for example, access to commercial exploitation from outside the family is not really 'seen' as a danger or as corrupting, but sexual exploitation is seen to be both.

Why do you think this might be?

Activity 2

The report notes that new media is met by public concern about their impact on society and anxiety leads to 'emotive calls for action' (2008, 3). It notes that some link children's use of the internet to 'violent and destructive behaviour in the young' (2008, 3). Concerns are also that 'excessive use' by children is at the expense of other activities and family interaction: 'As we increasingly keep our children at home because of fears for their safety outside – in what some see as a "risk-averse culture" – they will play out their developmental drives to socialize and take risks in the digital world' (2008, 3).

⇨

Example of research—Cont'd

- How do you see this in relation to genuine risk of children and young people's safety and harm and how much a reflection of 'risk averse culture'?
- How do you see this 'anxiety' in relation to the argument that it reflects parental:
  o desire to keep control of an arena they feel children and young people are more adept and socially skilled within?
  o fears of new kinds of new social interactions which they do not understand?

Does such fear become an arena that is an extension of other frameworks of fear, protection and safeguarding? On the one hand is the very real situation of children accessing links and material such as suicide sites, or pornography. On the other are the dynamics that create a national scare which obscures the complexity of a situation. The research helps unravel some of these dynamics to see some of the processes at work that create and reflect adult fear and anxiety.

One of the interesting things about the Byron review, for example, is the way in which children's capacity and skill being superior to the parent or guardian is framed. It is seen as something that means the child can escape the gate keeping and 'view' of the adult in much the same way that relates to fears of playing out or being unsupervised elsewhere. The following pieces of recent research help illuminate these adult attitudes further.

Example of research: parents and children

Livingstone and Bober (2005) undertook researching into children and young people's use of the internet to draw out issues for future research in the area. It combined a variety of methods including computer-assisted interviews with 1511 children and young people aged 9 to 19 along with focus group and family observation work. Livingstone and Bober's research drew conclusions concerning children's response that creates a more complex picture than that of the Byron report:

Table 6.1 Jones adapted from Livingstone and Bober (2005)

Children and young people	Parents
31% of daily and weekly users have received unwanted sexual messages online or by text	7% said they are aware that their child has received sexual comments
33% have received 'nasty comments' online or by text message	4% of parents said they are aware that their child has been bullied online

⇨

Example of research—Cont'd

Most of the children said they were aware, from media coverage, of the risks of meeting strangers they had made contact with online. Livingstone and Bober present the following statistics in relation to this area of concern:

Table 6.2 Jones adapted from Livingstone and Bober (2005)

Children and young people

46% said that they have given out personal information to someone that they met online

40% say that they have pretended about themselves online

30% have made an online acquaintance

8% say they have met face to face with someone whom they first met online. The vast majority of the 8% that had met someone face to face had told a friend or parent and the researchers were told that most went with a friend to the meeting.

Reflections on the research
Activity 1

The researchers make the following two comments in relation to these findings:

> Multivariate analyses show that social–psychological factors, family communication patterns and gender all play a role in the interaction risks that are taken by teens online.
>
> (Livingstone and Bober, 2005, 6)

> Offline family communication patterns and parental attitudes towards the internet and other media also had an impact on communication online by young people.
>
> (Livingstone and Bober, 2005, 6)

One way of reading this analysis is to say that there are many factors that combine in terms of 'safety' and 'risk', such as how and whether families communicate about risks connected with children and young people's use of the internet, or gender. One of the comments talks about the impact of 'family communication patterns and parental attitudes' on risk: what do you understand by *patterns* and *attitudes* here?

Activity 2

Consider the relationship between adult attitudes as reflected in the research findings and the ideas from Chapters 4 and 5 about adult stereotypes that view children as primarily vulnerable or incapable, rather than as agents in their own lives capable of making decisions and having the capacity to make judgements for themselves. Do you think these stereotypes relate to the findings?

The following example of research offers a further, contrasting perspective on the uses of the internet, attitudes and parental supervision.

Example of research: blogging and escaping the home

Research by Huffaker and Calvert (2005) offers a different perspective on the 'danger' of the internet compared to the 'safety' of the home environment. Their research indicated that adolescents often assume different identities or different identity qualities, are 'less inhibited' and develop relationships with strangers. Some research, for example, on the use of teenage blogging, has indicated that this can be positive, offering opportunities for self-discovery and self-validation (2005) and helps adolescents develop their concept of themselves.

Huffaker and Calvert conducted a content analysis of randomly selected blogs that were created and maintained by teenagers between 13 and 17. They note the role of internet communication in the shifting ways that developmental 'milestones' of adolescence are encountered. During this time they say that the processes involved in assuming a mature sexual identity are encountered by all youth, and 'these challenges may be particularly difficult for those who are gay, lesbian, bisexual, or transgendered', and that they may not be able to discuss this with those in their immediate environment – such as the family. Huffaker and Calvert assert:

> In a virtual world, where flexibility and anonymity are possible, adolescents may feel more comfortable expressing their sexual orientation and exploring their sexual identity beyond social prescriptions. In online forums, including weblogs, language is a key means through which sexual identity can be expressed and explored.

Table 6.3 Contingency table of sexual identity among male and female bloggers

	Total (n=70)	Male (n=35)	Female (n=35)
Relationships	49% (34)	25% (17)	25% (17)
Homosexuality	17% (12)	14% (10)	3% (2)

Some 17 per cent of male bloggers 'discussed a homosexual identity'. Huffaker and Calvert say that this suggests that male bloggers may be using blogs as a safe and comfortable environment to be honest, or even candid, about their sexual identity and feelings.

Unlike a private diary, discussing 'coming out' online can be empowering, as the blog author is aware that his posts can be read in the public sphere. They suggest that increased acceptance of homosexuality by certain subgroups, particularly youth, may make the disclosure of sexual orientation less of a risk than it has been

⇨

in the past: 'Disclosing one's sexual identity online may also provide a way for gay teens to find others who share their sexual identity. Taken together, our findings suggest that adolescents seek a continuity of representations of who they are, as well as a confirmation of those representations by their peers'.

Reflections on the research
Activity 1

How do you think these issues might relate to the vast difference between children and young people's use of the internet in terms of contact with people as presented in **Tables 6.1 and 6.2** and the use described in the 'Example of research: **Parents and Children Research**' above?

Activity 2

Discuss the relationship of parents wanting to regulate their sons' and daughters' sexuality by comparing the positive ways in which Huffaker and Calvert talk about internet usage compared with the 'Internet risk and the Byron review' comment:

> parents do not feel empowered to manage risks in the digital world in the same way that they do in the 'real' world (2008, 3).

How do adult ideas and practices concerning our fear of children affect children's lives?

The theme of children being fearful runs through a range of different areas of contemporary living. The US National Council on Crime and Delinquency commissioned a national opinion poll concerning public attitudes towards 'youth crime' and found that 91 per cent agreed with the statement 'Crime committed by young people is a major problem in our communities' (Krisberg and Marchionna, 2007). A 2004 study in England and Wales, funded by the Nuffield Foundation, found that 75 per cent of those polled believed that the number of young offenders had increased in the previous two years. Officially, the numbers of young offenders coming to police attention fell by 9 per cent over the same period. The report's conclusions drew from such statistics that the public has a more pessimistic view of youth crime than is justified by official crime statistics (Hough and Roberts, 2004).

Such attitudes have a presence in the way legislation is formulated, and in the way that the justice system is conducted. In addition, it is in the forefront of adult's minds and opinions, and is expressed in the way we interact with children and in the world we create for children to inhabit through the ways attitudes affect behaviour, rules and regulations. Restrictions are a primary way in which this area of attitude manifests, expresses and encourages itself. These restrictions surface in how laws are created which, for example, inhibit the way children access and use spaces such as neighbourhood streets. Such legislation also creates barriers, limits and inhibitions through formal and informal strictures in the relationships formed between adults and children. Some have argued that the UK's Crime and Disorder Act (1998) and the Anti-Social Behaviour Act (2003) are examples of such negative interaction between attitude and legislation. The Crime and Disorder Act removed the defence of 'doli incapax' from children aged between 10 and 14. Within that defence the prosecution had to prove that the child knew that what they had done was 'wrong'. Dowty comments that its removal 'had the effect of making children fully liable for their criminal actions from the age of 10' with no need to prove any level of understanding and making it 'one of the lowest ages of criminal responsibility in Western Europe' (2008, 20). This contrasts with the UNCRC's recommendation that 12 is the minimum age of criminal responsibility, and that this must also bear in mind issues concerning 'emotional, mental and intellectual maturity' (UNCRC, 2007). The Anti-Social Behaviour Act included provision for the dispersal of groups of young people in the street, and for giving individual children Anti-Social Behaviour Orders (ASBOs). Thomas (2007) cites the response of the campaign group Liberty to this legislation saying that the UK government was in danger of making it a 'crime to be a child' (Verkaik 2005). This is linked by him to the Council of Europe's direct criticism of the UK's legislation. Their comments say that ASBOs aim at 'reducing urban nuisance', but that their primary effect was to bring young people into the criminal justice system, and to place them 'often enough behind bars without [them] necessarily having committed a recognisable criminal offence' (Council of Europe, 2005, para 83). He also refers to the *Independent* newspaper's editorial commentary on how adult attitudes and legislation can connect in a way that damages children: 'the reflex to slap ASBOs on unruly children is related to that recent bout of hysteria about the prevalence of kids wearing "hoodies" in shopping centres' (*Independent*, 20 June, 2005 cited in Thomas, 2007, 6). Thomas goes on to echo the editorial's view that such legislation is an avoidance of looking at the wider responsibilities of society in relation to children. This includes issues such as the provision of facilities for children out of school, and the inappropriate attempt that ASBOs represent in 'asking the criminal justice system to resolve social problems of low incomes, inequality and blocked ambitions' (2007, 6). In bringing these comments together Thomas illustrates very effectively one of the key points of this chapter. He is showing how adult attitudes create the impetus for legislation that is rooted in adult prejudice and stereotyping. The legislation is fuelled by attitudes that do not try to view the complex issues in children's lives, to look at the legislation from the children's perspective or to act in any way that looks towards their interests. Hence the attitudes are creating a system that is criticized by the Council of Europe for criminalizing 'the young' when no 'recognisable' crime has been committed. Kemshall (2008) has described an aspect of the phenomenon of positioning and seeing children as fearful as a 'distortion' of youth, arguing that children and young people have become a 'prism' through which adults try to see all the ills of society.

What does research reveal about the impact of the attitudes that drive the creation of these phenomena? What can we discover about the way they relate, not only to policy formation, but also to the ways adults and children relate to each other in their daily lives?

The discourses within the media are clearly identified within the research findings. People do not have very much direct experience of 'youth crime', but the research indicates that they cite awareness through media forms. The media is cited as a key source in the creation of an atmosphere of fear. In the Nuffield research cited earlier, for example, respondents were asked 'What makes you think that the number of young offenders has increased?' Some 64 per cent of respondents claimed that media reports had informed their views, though they had little direct experience in their own lives.

Fear, communities and adult false perceptions

In looking at fear of children and young people, two pieces of research from Scotland can help to examine the relationship between projected adult fears or 'crime-related anxiety' and the actual levels of recorded crime. The research excerpts will explore the detrimental impact these adult fears and projections have on children's, and on adult's, lives.

Example of research: crime anxiety versus actual crime

Recent research looked at perceptions of over 1500 adults concerning youth crime in Scotland (Anderson et al., 2005) and the UK (Hough and Roberts, 2004). In the UK, 42 per cent believed that half of all crimes were committed by young people. Official statistics suggest that the figure is more likely to be somewhere between 10 and 20 per cent. Two-thirds estimated the percentage of youth crime involving violence at over 40 per cent. Police records of the numbers of young offenders being cautioned or convicted for violent crimes suggest a much lower figure of 20 per cent. In Scotland the vast majority, over 70 per cent, thought that youth crime was higher than ten years ago, with 0.5 per cent thinking it was lower. The research analysis compares this with police recorded crime statistic, and, whilst noting that it is difficult to estimate the actual level of youth crime because of the nature of recording incidents compared to people's actual experience, they refer to recorded crime statistics lowering significantly in a 'largely downward trajectory since the early 1990s' (2005, 23) and link this to other such analysis and comment about the disparity between felt attitude in this area and recorded incidences (Hough and Roberts, 2004; Anderson et al., 2002):

> Despite evidence to the contrary from crime statistics, there is widespread perception (across all sections of the adult population) that the level of youth crime is higher than it was ten years ago.
>
> (Anderson et al., 2005, 32)

The research asked people whether they had been directly affected by different types of crime. Here the findings were that between 3 and 4 per cent said they were affected 'a great deal' by groups of young people hanging round in the street, vandalism, graffiti or other deliberate damage to property and problems caused by young people who have been drinking, with 85 to 86 per cent saying that they had been directly affected 'not very much' or 'not at all' (2005, 25).

The research interprets this as a 'disjunction of sorts between such views and the proportion of adults who say they have been directly affected by various types of youth crime and disorder' (2005, 27). The research also investigated what it termed the 'indirect consequences' of such a disjunction – what it calls crime-related anxiety – which is not related to actual crime figures or incidences but 'the extent to which adults *worry* about becoming the victim or crime . . . and the extent to which they alter their behaviour as a result of anxieties about young people in public places' (2005, 27). These worries were greater in those who had little or no contact with young people.

⇨

For the areas referred to before – of hanging around the street and for vandalism and graffiti – the figures for people worried a 'great deal' or 'quite a lot' were between 42 and 44 per cent (2005, 27).

The research looked at the specific impacts of such attitudes; for example, at the extent to which adults 'modify their behaviour as a result of anxieties about young people'. In response to imagining a situation in which they simply had to walk past a group of teenagers in order to get to a shop, 6 per cent said they would avoid walking past them and over half of all the adults said that they would be worried to some degree. Women and older people were more likely than younger people to be worried and those in areas of 'greater deprivation' were twice as likely as those in areas of less deprivation to be very worried or would avoid walking past them (2005, 29).

Reflections on the research
Activity

One of the key themes the research highlights in its conclusions is that:

> many adults had little or no contact with young people. For example, 43% of respondents said they had no contact or less than one contact a month with children aged 11 to 14 involving chatting or talking.
>
> (2005, 43)

The research considers from such statistics:

> One of the consequences of the recent focus on youth crime and 'yob culture' has been as 'othering' of young people – a tendency to regard them as 'a tribe apart', distinct and differentiated from adult society. . . . it should . . . be noted that a sizeable minority of adults have little or no social contact between the ages of 11 and 24. The results of this study suggest that such contact does matter . . . contact with young people are consistently more likely to have negative views of the young.
>
> (2005, 33)

What factors, apart from lack of contact, within the research do you see as contributing to this 'othering'?

Within the legal system some research has indicated that children are treated in ways that work to keep them silenced, and to be passive receivers of adult blame and exclusion. There are increasing examples of effective policies and practice that challenge such attitudes in areas such as youth justice, and that examine the harmful ways of working with children that they result in.

However, a constant theme within much of the research in this book is the tension between intentions and policies that attempt to value children and not treat them as 'other', and the resistances to their effective implementation. The research undertaken by Kilkelly (2008) shows this tension at work in Irish Children Courts.

Example of research: children courts

Nine hundred and forty-four Irish Children Court proceedings were observed and analysed in four major regional centres. The standards the proceedings were measured against were rooted in the UNCRC and to specific guidelines that attempt to be inclusive and to protect children. One example of this is that 'every child has a right to understand and participate in criminal proceedings against him/her and that the court has a duty to facilitate exercise of this right' (Kilkelly, 2008, 50).

The research showed a picture that could hardly be contrasted more starkly with this framework of inclusivity, protection, understanding and participation.

In the majority of cases (55%) the research observation and analysis of actual Children's Court proceedings found:

- no communication of any kind took place between judges and young people;
- the judge did not greet the young person on arrival into court;
- the judge did not speak to them during any stage of the process;
- the judge did not explain when the proceedings were concluded;
- questions about the young person were directed to their solicitor and the young person was referred to as 'he' or 'she' as if they were not present.

When interaction did take place in the other 45 per cent, it was 'minimal', involving a 'basic greeting' with the young person being asked a few details such as which school they went to.

The research concludes that court procedures had not been adapted to take into account the age and understanding of young people. In the 'vast majority' of the cases:

- normal legal jargon and explanations were used, such as 'electing trial' in the Circuit Court;
- little, or no, attempt was made to adapt explanations to facilitate any understanding before questions were asked, resulting in 'blank faces' or children looking to family or solicitors for support;
- on the small number of occasions when young people were asked to explain what they understood by a comment or decision made within the proceedings they were simply unable to do so.

⇨

The detailed observations include the following comments:

> [During the proceedings] young people . . . were observed staring at the floor or ceiling or chatting with family members. Some did not realize their case was over until the next case was called, prompting them to get up and leave the court.
>
> (2008, 51)

> On rare occasions the interaction between the young person and the judge was aggressive with the young person being ordered about, insulted or reprimanded about his/her dress or posture.
>
> (2008, 51)

The report also notes that in many situations the children were physically placed in a way that made interaction of any sort, even of hearing what was happening, difficult.

Reflections on the research
Activity 1

The research concludes by pointing to the inadequacy, or absence, of any effort to ensure children being dealt with in a way that takes account of their maturity, intellectual or emotional capacities.

How do you see this absence in relation to children being silenced?

Why might adults not permit children to understand what was happening to them in this way, despite guidelines and policy to the contrary?

Activity 2

Davies (2005) has linked together such attitudes and policy to illustrate the negative impact they have on both adults and children. He argues that a 'strategy' is being developed, based on deliberately exploiting popular tensions, fears and prejudice:

> The result is to encourage blanket demonising and dehumanising of a whole generational segment of the population by resort to, and then the continuous recycling of, labels such as 'yob' and 'feral youth'. In order to turn the full weight of the state against these demons, disproportionate public and policy responses are then endorsed, which involves serious distortion of the operation of judicial and law enforcement procedures.
>
> (2005, 7)

How do you see the processes described within Kilkelly's findings relate to:

- challenging, or maintaining, adult stereotypes of children as threats?
- Davies' points about distorting justice procedures in the light of stereotyping?

Table 6.4 Key tensions Jones from Reay and Lucey (2000) and Holland et al. (2007)

at risk	a risk to others
deviant delinquent	passive victim
vulnerable, incompetent,	anti-social, dangerous,
in need of protection	adults need protection
and supervision	from them

Researchers have pointed to the paradox and tension present within the kinds of attitudes revealed within the research explored so far in this chapter. Reay and Lucey (2000), for example, concluded from their research that 'relevant discourses of social exclusion position such children as both "at risk" and a risk to others'. They are portrayed as a mixture of deviant delinquent and passive victim. Weller (2007) and Holland et al. (2007), following research into the relationship between children, social capital and neighbourhood, observed that children are frequently portrayed as vulnerable, incompetent and in need of protection from the possible dangers of town and city streets. However, they point out that, at the same time, they are allowed to go out and meet up in public areas that are often regarded as intimidating and threatening.

Aynsley-Green, England's Commissioner for Children, has brought these paradoxical views together when he commented: 'whilst children are often sentimentalised, young people are "demonised", and 70% of press cuttings are negative' (2005). Anderson et al. place these media scares and people's attitudes to them as 'part of age-old stories in which children and young people are portrayed as both "angels" and "devils" . . . or simultaneously viewed both as threat (in that they symbolize social change and the dismantling of the existing order) and as hope (in that they represent symbolize the possibilities of a new beginning' (2005, 35). The following research brings together aspects of both stands of this chapter: attitudes concerning adult fear for children and fear of children.

Example of research: adults' attitudes towards contact with children and young people

The research was conducted in Scotland (Scotland's Commissioner for Children and Young People/Rocket Science, 2007) and looked at adult attitudes towards children.

⇨

The results state that when most people were asked to describe general experiences with children, both positive and negative, most people tended to focus on the negative not the positive. Positive experiences were more readily made by those with more regular contact with children and young people and these often related to the pleasure gained through seeing the personal and social development of individuals over time.

The report concludes that the contexts in which positive and negative experiences took place were distinctly different. Negative ones tended to take place with large numbers of young people in what it calls 'uncontrolled environments', while positive ones were in 'structured environments' or on a one-to-one basis.

The research examined adults' attitudes towards general contact with children and young people in public spaces, the likelihood of helping children and young people in danger or distress, and views on working or volunteering with them. The attitudes towards different age groups of children, from very young children through to teenagers, were also explored.

The conclusions of the report can be viewed as at the heart of the discussion of attitudes in this chapter; indeed, they echo many of the terms we are exploring. They state them in the following way.

Overall, there were some consistent themes across all areas of the research. These were particularly in relation to:

> Adult's fear of accusations of harming children and young people;
>
> The reluctance of men to have contact, help or work with children and young people for fear of society's suspicion of their own motives;
>
> The fear of teenagers; and
>
> The perceived power of children and young people.
>
> . . . the fear of accusations of harming children was the main barrier identified by survey respondents and focus group participants in terms of having contact with children and young people or working with them. It was also identified by focus group participants as one of the main reasons they would hesitate to help a child or young person in danger or distress in the hypothetical scenarios.
>
> (2007, 2)

The issue was unpicked in the focus groups and the report concludes that the participants gave three main factors underpinning this fear:

> A fear that young people might use accusations as a way of getting attention or manipulating adults (for example, in order to force them to buy drink);
>
> A belief that because of the seriousness of accusations, adults will be considered guilty until proven innocent, and the support provided to the accused will be minimal; and
>
> A belief that being accused of harming children was one of the worst accusations imaginable, and one which your reputation might not recover from despite them being unfounded.
>
> (2007, 2–3)

⇨

Example of research—Cont'd

The report also says that it is not clear 'where these fears have originated' as few of the respondents were personally aware of situations involving false accusations, though a higher proportion said they 'were aware' of stories in the media. It states 'the fear of being accused of paedophilia is quite clearly at the forefront of men's minds when considering whether to have contact with children. This fear was so strong that many focus group participants said it would make them think twice about approaching a lost child to help them, despite a relatively high proportion saying they would intervene in the survey.'

The report says that when asked about how to encourage people to have more contact there were very few suggestions:

> The barriers to overcome are fairly substantial, particularly given the high level of fear of accusations and concerns about being labelled a paedophile. The actual risk to the individual may be small.
>
> (2007, 3)

Reflections on the research
Activity

Key themes identified by other researchers included the idea that attitudes are paradoxical. These included:

- children are seen both as 'at risk' and as the opposite – a risk to others;
- children are portrayed as a paradoxical mix of deviant delinquent and passive victim.

How do you see the research findings above in relation to these tensions and paradoxes?

Interview with David McNeill about Rocket Science's research

David McNeill, Rocket Science UK Ltd.

Phil Jones: How do you see the role of research such as yours in relation to attitudes towards children?

David McNeill: While young people in Scotland consistently call for more activities, there are not enough adults prepared to take both work and volunteering roles with them. The research helped to provide evidence on the factors which influence adults' decisions on whether to have contact, help, work or volunteer with children and young people. The Commissioner hopes that this report will stimulate a full public debate about how to bridge the divide between the generations, and establish a framework for attractive activities that are stimulating, safe and fun for all involved.

Phil Jones: **What did you discover about further directions for research from this experience?**

David McNeill: It was surprising to see the fear of accusations of harming children and young people being identified as such a strong barrier to contact. In 2008, the Commissioner undertook further qualitative research to:

- explore in more detail issues related to the fear of accusations of harming children and young people, and to identify ways to alleviate these fears, enabling more adults to have positive contact with children and young people; and
- explore people's views of what is needed to minimize the negative impact (or perception of the negative impact) of regulations and make people feel more positive about working with children and young people or setting up activities for them.

This research is due for publication shortly.

An area not fully explored in this research that merits further investigation is in relation to gender and attitudes towards contact with children and young people. There was an identified cultural stereotype than men could pose danger to children and young people and therefore their motives for contact are more likely to be called into question.

The impact of adult fears

Research such as that undertaken by the Scotland's Commissioner can be examined to show that adult fear of teenagers becomes used in particular ways. Here the cultural breadth of the assumption that potentially all children are vulnerable to abuse by all adults is combined with the idea that children are dangerous, deceptive, and will create lies as a way of harming innocent adults who are trying to help them. Here conflated are the themes of opportunities involving help or care from an adult to a child being closely allied to its opposite: harm.

Kemshall makes the point that 'social problems are reframed as crime problems and crime control strategies are increasingly deployed to manage intractable social ills' (2008, 22). This is particularly so in response to children and young people in marginalized and excluded communities, and that the 'individualistic and blame-laden language of risk transforms social and collective risks into individual ones' (2008, 23). Hence a society need not look to overall problems and issues such as how inequality, poverty and inequality relate to young people's experiences, and to try to look at actions to support young people. Instead, it can keep viewing them as 'other', as fearful and to see them in terms of blame and undeserving of any understanding. In this way they can be 'excluded, marginalized and demonized' (2008, 23).

How can attitudes be challenged and changed?

In the light of this phenomenon, what ways are there of looking at how adults and children can relate?

Children themselves reveal more complex responses than the stereotypes and projections and anxieties that adults respond to them with. Reay and Lucey concluded from their research, for example:

> relevant discourses of social exclusion position such children as both 'at risk' and a risk to others. They are portrayed as a mixture of deviant delinquent and passive victim. In contrast, this research study found that children have a reflexive awareness of the places they inhabit which recognizes the estates as harsh and restricting, yet the same time encompasses more positive feelings of identification and belonging. Most children shared a sense of feeling 'at home', but one which was infused with both a recognition of the stigma associated with 'sink' estates and a fascinated horror with regard to the behaviour of a delinquent minority.
>
> (2000, 92–3)

A consistent theme from a number of pieces of research lies in conclusions that such adult misconceptions need to be challenged. This is seen to redress the fuelling of negative images, concepts and prejudices that focus on a stereotyped notion of children and young people. In turn, this is linked to a need to redress the kinds of policies and practices such as ASBOs in the UK, which can result from this culturally held and maintained vilification and othering (see Chapter 3) or the need for greater clarity that challenges held positions that are unhelpful.

Research by Mesie et al. (2007), for example, indicates the need for changes in perceptions and the ways in which safeguarding children is seen: developing a shared understanding of what constitutes behaviours in adults that need preventing, what constitutes abuse and defining safeguarding was 'easily the biggest challenge' for society (2007, 111). Their recommendations include actions that involved challenging the ambivalence of health services, schools and public perceptions regarding neglect and abuse: making sure that parents and carers know what looking after children and safeguarding means, and that children also know what safeguarding means (2007, 111). They identify the need to engage with 'potential obstacles' such as cultural issues concerning privacy, and 'the way in which people may think of safeguarding mainly in relation to services as opposed to individual and community attitudes towards children' (2007, 112). This is echoed by other commentators who argue that the key contemporary challenge in this area is to resolve the tensions in adult attitudes between public expressions of fear for children's safety and ambivalence towards the nature, extent and right of those outside of the family to intervene on behalf of children. Walker, for example, in describing how these inherent contradictions are reflected in legislation and guidance, comments that until they are resolved,

> there will continue to be children whose childhoods reflect a different societal value from the child-centred, children-as-precious view put forward in the official vision for the future of safeguarding children.
>
> (2008, 151)

In the report 'Youth crime and youth justice: public opinion in England and Wales', Hough and Roberts (2003), as with other research examined earlier, found that public fear of young criminals is greatly exaggerated. They conclude that:

- in a world that equates government with 'spin', those best placed to inform the public – government researchers and statisticians – have increasingly less credibility;
- this puts a particular obligation on reform groups, academic criminologists and the youth justice system itself, to address public misperceptions.

Their research notes the following conclusions:

- Media representations of youth crime focus on violent crimes and report specific examples of the worst kinds of juvenile offenders.
- These are not the cases that appear in youth courts on a daily basis.
- The public need to be reminded that behind the headlines about 'feral rat boys', there is a large number of young people who have become involved in the criminal justice system as a result of a wide variety of factors, not all of which are under their control (2003, 2004).

A report by Anderson et al. notes an ambivalence towards young people from adults – and considers the following possibilities:

- Adults can be divided between those who are sympathetic and those who are hostile – on the basis of experience and circumstance.
- Adults make conscious or unconscious distinctions between young people who are known to them and those who are not – a highly critical view of young people as a whole can coexist with warm attitudes towards one's own, grandchildren or those of neighbours.
- Adults make distinctions based on criteria such as social class, ethnicity or other characteristics such as those in rural communities being suspicious about the children of incomers (2005, 33).

They draw conclusions from their research that parallel Hough and Roberts:

- Policy should avoid reinforcing stereotypes of and suspicion of young people.
- This will have the effect of reducing contact further.
- Explicit attempts to foster inter-generational links (2005, 35).

Weller et al. (2007) examined children's experiences of travelling to school and to a wide range of activities outside the home – from formal clubs to hanging out in the park. They bring together aspects of the two themes in this chapter: fear of and fear for children. Their findings offer a way forward to rethinking how we see children and young people and towards issues of young people's role in the idea of 'community' and their participation in this community:

- Contrary to popular opinion children play a key role in strengthening local communities and making people feel safe in their neighbourhoods.
- Much panic today about childhood in urban areas is based on a very partial picture.
- Previous theories that see social networks as mostly determined by parents ignore the crucial contribution made by children.
- Children are active – both indirectly and directly – in forging neighbourly relationships and connections for their parents.
- Many parents suggested that they had established more networks and friendships in the local area through their children than by any other means. This contact came via antenatal classes, the nursery and the primary school, or through their children's friends' families.

The findings were from a three-year study involving some 600 children and 80 parents in five contrasting areas – two inner London boroughs, an outer London suburb, a new town in the south-east England, and a city in the Midlands. The researchers found that the more parents were involved in the lives of their neighbours, the more freedom they gave their children. At the same time, the more social networks children have in a neighbourhood, the greater parents' confidence in the safety of that area. Many parents questioned were often torn between wishing to protect their children and wanting them to be 'streetwise'. Parents acknowledged that their children had much less freedom to roam or explore the neighbourhood than they enjoyed. They saw this as a problem, and generally wanted the youngsters to be out and about more. The research suggests that when parents allow their children to roam, their classmates' parents draw from that confidence. This in turn impacts upon their classmates' freedom of action. Weller (2007) concludes: 'On the one hand, children are frequently portrayed as vulnerable, incompetent, and in need of protection from the possible dangers of town and city streets. On the other, those allowed to go out and meet up in public areas are often regarded as intimidating and anti-social.'

Activities

The following activities are designed to help reflect back on some of the key concerns over the chapter as a whole.

Chapter activity 1

Anderson et al. concluded from their research that:

> public perceptions of young people and youth crime are a valuable alternative index of the problem, in that they tell us something important about how our communities function and about the collective resources that can be drawn upon when problems with young people arise. In other words, public attitudes in this area should be seen as helping to constitute, and not simple reflecting, the problem of youth crime.
>
> (2005, 35)

How do you see the work of Weller (2007) and that contained in the 'Examples of Research: **adults' attitudes towards contact with children and young people**' in relation to the idea that research into attitudes can help to see both what the problems in attitudes are and what 'resources' a community has to help combat adult attitudes?

Chapter activity 2

Go through all the boxed examples of research in this chapter and identify issues where adults are 'gatekeepers' of children. Reflect or discuss what aspects of these reflect adult attitudes and fears primarily, rather than the needs of children, and which you consider are directly necessary to safeguard children.

Discuss which you consider are seeing children as incapable (as discussed in Chapter 4) rather than as capable in their own right.

Summary

This chapter has:

- looked at the ways adult attitudes regarding fear for children reflects genuine concerns for children and the need for safeguarding;
- examined ways in which adult fear can also reflect adult projections and preoccupations rather than real needs to protect or safeguard children;
- looked at the relationship between research that offers insights into the way adult fears can confine children and that sees them as primarily vulnerable and needy rather than as individuals who can discern and make judgements;
- reviewed research that examined ideas and practices concerning adult fears of children and young people and the ways in which this reflects adult anxieties rather than the actual situations of children and young people;
- reviewed research that examined ideas and practices that looked at how negative stereotyping of young people as fearful is being challenged.

Further reading

Bolzan, N. (2008) '"Kids are like that!" Community attitudes to young people', National Youth Affairs Research Scheme, Commonwealth, State and Territory Government of Australia. Online: www.facs.gov.au/internet/facsinternet.nsf/aboutfacs/programs/youth-kids_that.htm.

A report on a community survey, in-depth interviews with young people and focus groups with groups within communities about perceptions of, and attitudes towards young people.

Kehily, M. and Montgomery, H. (2004) 'Innocence and experience: a historical approach to childhood and sexuality', in Kehily M. (ed) *An Introduction to Childhood Studies*. Maidenhead: Open University Press.

A historical perspective on issues concerning the social and cultural factors concerning ideas of childhood and innocence created in opposition to an adult's world seen as dangerous and corrupting.

Moss, D. (2008a) 'Children who offend', in Jones, P., Moss, D., Tomlinson, P. and Welch, S. (eds) *Childhood: Services and Provision for Children*. Harlow: Pearson.

A review of how children's behaviour has come to be defined as a crime, and an analysis of the factors that shape ideas about crime and childhood. The chapter explores the development of debates that have created provision in relation to youth justice and challenges attitudes and their impact on children's lives.

Research details

Internet risk and the Byron review (2008)

Report commissioned by UK government. Included call for evidence with reponses from 350 children aged between 5 and 18 years, focus groups with forty-eight parents and forty-two children segmented by age of child, socio-economic status, geographical location.

Byron, T. (2008) 'Safer Children in a Digital World: The Report of the Byron review'. Online: www.dfes.gov.uk/byronreview (accessed 12 June 2008).

Parents and children

Livingstone and Bober (2005) undertook researching into children and young people's use of the internet to draw out issues for future research in the area. It combined a variety of methods including computer assisted interviews with 1511 children and young people aged 9–19 along with focus group and family observation work.

Livingstone, S. and Bober, M. (2005) 'UK Children Go Online: final report of key project findings'. London School of Economics and Political Science. LSE Research online.

Blogging and escaping the home

Peer-reviewed journal. Huffaker and Calvert (2005) combined focus groups and surveys to look at experiences of internet use and practice among children.

Huffaker, D. A. and Calvert, S. L. (2005) 'Gender, identity and language use in teenage blogs', *Journal of Computer-Mediated Communication*, 10, 2, article 1.

Crime anxiety versus actual crime

National research funded by the Scottish Government, Scottish Executive Education Department through survey of perceptions of over 1500 adults concerning youth crime in Scotland (Anderson et al., 2005).

Anderson, S., Bromley, C. and Given, L. (2005) 'Public attitudes towards young people and youth crime in Scotland: findings from the 2004 Scottish Social Attitudes Survey'. Scottish Executive Education Department.

Children courts

The research was funded by the Irish Research Council for the Humanities and Social Sciences in order to establish the extent to which the Children Courts were operating in relation to national and international standards. It was carried out in 2003–04 in Dublin, Cork, Limerick and Waterford and 944 cases were observed over fifty-two court days. The study observed the physical environment of the court, the positioning of the parties and the interaction between them during the proceedings, including dialogue. Forms were used to record information in each case and then overall analysis was made.

Kilkelly, U. (2008) 'Youth courts and children's rights: the Irish experience', *Youth Justice*, 8, 1, 39–56.

Adults' attitudes towards contact with children and young people

The research was conducted in Scotland (Scotland Commissioner for Children and Young people, 2007) by a national survey of adults, followed by focus group exploring in depth the survey responses.

Scotland's Commissioner for Children and Young People (2007) 'Adults' attitudes towards contact with children and young people'. Report Scotland's Commissioner for Children and Young People and Rocket Science.

Unseen and Unheard or Seen and Heard? Participation and Exclusion

7

Chapter Outline

Introduction and key questions

Should the views of children be taken into account in what happens to them? Do adults listen to children? If they do, is what they hear of any value? This chapter will look at whether we are changing from a world where children are seen but not heard, to one where their voices are included and acknowledged. It will look at whether services such as schools or hospitals actually act on children's views, or whether they create a veneer of involvement whilst keeping tight hold of real power and control.

This chapter will examine the ways in which a child's rights perspective has begun to challenge traditional ideas and practices about participation. It will look at what research is revealing about what happens when children are involved in decision making and the idea that they can be agents in their own lives rather than being treated as the property of their parents.

- How and why do adults make decisions that shape children's worlds for them?
- What impact does adult decision making have on children's lives?
- What ideas and practices have been developed concerning children's participation?
- How has research explored the practice and impact of children's participation in decision making?

How and why do adults make decisions that shape children's worlds for them?

A number of reports and research initiatives show the effects of children inhabiting a world created for them by adults: a world that often only reflects adult ideas and preoccupations about childhood. This environment is usually defined and regulated by practices devised and carried out by adults, with little or no reference to children's own accounts of their experiences and lives – whether this be of their own bodies, feelings, hopes or troubles.

As this chapter will show, children and adults currently live in a world where children are deemed unable to make decisions, or where a child's abdominal pain is evaluated by their parent's opinions about the pain. Some service providers such as hospitals or local authorities have attempted change. However, in some of these initiatives research indicates that children are being asked for their opinions, but then no changes occur because their views threaten adult power. On the other hand, research is revealing effective ways to engage children in consultation and participation. These can have a real impact: resulting in changes in the services they use, or that involve them in decisions about their lives and what happens to them.

Article 12 in the United Nations Convention on the Rights of the Child says that governments: 'Shall assure to the child who is capable of forming his or her own views the right to express those views freely in all matters affecting the child, the views of the child being given due weight in accordance with the age and maturity of the child' (1989, 12.1).

The *Rights of Us* (2005) echoes these UNCRC concerns. This statement was the outcome of a seminar organized with children and young people developing from the UK's ESRC (Economic and Social Research Council) meetings about policy, practice and research to redress children and young people's social exclusion. The document, written by children, looked at issues relating to their lived experience in relation to the UNCRC and identified key areas for change. It highlights what it describes as 'what young people want'. These concern: being listened to, having their opinions valued and treated with respect, and being actively involved in decisions that affected their lives. Specific points include:

> Disabled young people not being allowed to make decisions about their health and welfare.
>
> *Young person from Birmingham*

> Adults jump to assumptions in making key decisions that affect people's lives without talking to them.
>
> *Young person from Liverpool*

> Why can't young people work alongside adult professionals?
>
> *Young person from Durham*
> (*Rights of Us*, 2005, 2)

Many years on from the UNCRC it is worth asking why children and young people should still feel the need to voice such concerns and demands?

Most children's lives are spent between home, school and the streets or spaces in their local community. These include day centres, surgeries, hospitals or shops. They also inhabit other arenas such as the internet, or create and access communities though electronic communication by Facebook or texting. The ways in which they live and are silenced within these areas are affected by many forces that connect with different aspects of adult attitudes. On a micro level these include the impact of the people with whom they share their spaces, or those whose immediate day-to-day decision making and attitudes have a powerful impact on the ways any child is allowed, or permitted to live, in spaces such as their home, school, street or playground. On a macro level, forces such as policy making in areas such as education, the law or housing relate to children's participation. In addition, forces such as poverty, sexism and racism have an impact on the way children are heard or silenced.

In all of these spheres, from home to school, from policy making to poverty, adult decisions, opinions and voices have shaped, formed and ruled children's lives and the way they live, or are permitted to live. For generations, in many societies, the idea that a child should have a role to play in deciding about their world, what happens to themselves and to other children, or that they should have a voice in making decisions about adults has been anathema. As a result, children have found themselves in an adult-centred or adult-centric world.

Concepts such as that children can hold valid views and that they should be given weight in making decisions about their own lives, or on the lives of people around them often face direct and indirect opposition. Direct opposition might lie in laws about making decisions for themselves about their bodies. Indirect opposition might be found in practices that ask for children's opinions about schools or policies, but then, in reality, do nothing with those opinions if they challenge what adults want to hear, or do. Within areas such as family life or professional practice in health or education, part of the infrastructure of the way relationships are formed, or daily life is conducted, are long-held views that children:

- are the property of adults who make decisions for them;
- are incapable;
- are a danger to themselves or others, if left to decision making.

Some researchers have commented that these attitudes have an impact on a macro level to do with the ways in which children, when they become young people able to participate in democracy by voting, have become disenfranchised by this adult-centric environment from wanting to be involved:

> In the USA, as in Britain, young people are increasingly turning away from traditional political processes. This has been shown most dramatically in the extremely low turnouts at the Presidential election in the USA in 2000 (51.3%) and the British General election in 2001 (59%) – both all time lows. The respective levels for young people aged 18–24 were just 28% and 39%.
>
> (Cutler, 2002, 1)

On a micro level, research has shown that in family life, and in their day-to-day use of children's services, the desire of adults to hold on to decision making has a detrimental impact on children's lives. The impact of adult decision making and actions can be positive for children. However, research has shown that the ways in which adult's speak for, decide about and determine the lives of children can be deeply problematic and harmful.

What impact does adult decision making have on children's lives?

Recent research exposes the ways in which organizations automatically, and often unconsciously, only give real attention to the needs, voices and decisions of the adults who care for, or work with, children. The following 'Example of research' illustrates some of the many negative effects of this absence of attention on children's daily lives and their prospects for happy and healthy lives.

Example of research: children – seen and heard in health?

Bower et al. conducted a systematic review of evidence concerning 'the effectiveness of interventions for child and adolescent mental health problems' (2001, 373) in primary healthcare. They reviewed services for children ranging from sleep problems to recurrent abdominal pain, from children and families dealing with bereavement through to what are termed 'behaviour disorders'. I re-examined their findings looking at the ways in which the parental voice, compared to the child's voice, was represented in their review of research. The following are samples of the prevalent ways in which findings from different pieces of research were presented:

> In Finney's second study of the treatment of children with recurrent abdominal pain, parents were again satisfied with brief treatment.

> The outcomes of the health visitor's work showed that mother's ratings of problem severity reduced significantly over time, as did the General Health Questionnaire scores of parents whose children were being managed.

> Parents reported satisfaction with treatment and there were significant reductions in child behaviour problems.

> Coverley et al's (1995) uncontrolled study evaluated a single-session, 60-minute psychiatric evaluation for frequently attending mothers with children with psychiatric disorders. The session involved problem exploration and behavioural strategies. The session was rated positively by parents (although only 62% of those offered appointments attended). Mothers reported reduced problems in their children and the session was associated with a reduction in consultation rates.

> (Bower et al., 2001, 378–9: list of sources, Finney et al., 1989; Appleton et al., 1988; Finney et al., 1991; Coverley, 1995)

⇨

Example of research—Cont'd

Reflections on the research

In this research is revealed the ways in which the child's voice is hardly recognized and included in the language and conceptual frameworks within the review of research into child and adolescent health.

Here the research routinely reports parents' satisfaction about children's abdominal pain with no reference to the child's account or evaluation; children are 'managed' and the effectiveness of the intervention in a 'problem' is evaluated by mothers, or parents and whether they have 'satisfaction' with the 'treatment' of their children. In the account of Coverley, for example, the sessions for children with 'psychiatric disorders' are reported only in terms of the parents' ratings and mothers' reports on their children.

Activity

Mårtenson et al. (2007) echo this critique in their review of decision making in medical contexts, concluding that most research in decision-making competence in healthcare concerns adults' considerations made in 'the best interests' of the child, rather than any decision making made by, or involving, the children themselves.

How might this practice of parents deciding in the 'best interest' of the child relate to these reviews, where only the adult perspective is reported on by the professionals involved?

Consultant child and adolescent psychiatrist Maskey (2002, 599) talks about the negative impact on children's health of the ways in which priority is given to adult rather than children's voices, and how professional practice disenfranchises the child's representation of themselves from the family doctor's attention.

Key points from Maskey's critique

- In dealing with children, services prioritize parent and carer accounts, opinions and values over those of children themselves.
- This can lead to service providers distorting the way they engage with children, by adults relating to each other, not to the child.
- This can result in services neglecting children by not seeing them, hearing or respecting their experience or point of view, and not working with their needs and wants in an effective way (Maskey, 2002).

Maskey critiques the research of Kroenke (2002) and Gask and Underwood (2002) in looking at the variety of psychological difficulties presented by patients in general practice. He points out that in their research no mention is made of the many children seen both in general practice and by paediatricians, 'who have primarily mental health problems, psychological factors associated with their physical illness (such as diabetes management), or medically unexplained symptoms (such as recurrent abdominal pain)' (Maskey, 2002, 599).

He goes on to comment that the estimation of the prevalence of psychiatric disorders in young people in the United Kingdom made by the Office for National Statistics is 10 per cent of all children, with the figure increasing appreciably in inner cities, saying that, 'only one in five of these attend mental health services for children and adolescents. Some evidence exists that family doctors can provide effective treatment for this group' (2002, 599). He connects this to the issue of adult voices being given attention and children's voices being silenced, observing that children are in the unique position of being presented to their family doctors by parents, rather than seeking help themselves, and that this makes them vulnerable.

He argues that the emphasis on parental representation can lead to results such as children's needs not being met, or being misdiagnosed.

Example of research: researching children's interruptions

O'Reilly's (2006) small-scale research analysed videotapes of a number of different family therapy sessions to investigate how children's communications were treated by adults within therapy sessions. She looked at how the children's interruptions were responded to by family members and by the therapists, using a qualitative approach to contextualize each incidence. She found that therapists often ignored the child's interruptions and parental responses included:

- 'Be quiet' (parent)
- 'Shut up' (parent)
- 'Oi' (parent)
- 'No Kevin, wait' (parent)
- 'You've had your say' (parent) (2006, 558–60).

The following example is an excerpt from one of the transcripts of the videotapes analysed. The research describes the therapy session as considering the family's

⇨

Example of research—Cont'd

troubles communicating about feelings, and points out the ways that the interruptions by the child, Lee, are treated as negative, being ignored by the family therapist himself. Even when the child uses the therapist's name directly, 'Joe', family member Steve tells him to shut up, and his father tells Lee to shut up and then to wait:

Family therapist:	Which, which is kind of oh, you know, brothers and sisters might hate to admit they care
Lee:	Joe
Steve:	Shut up
Family therapist:	But then, Steve didn't want to know. He was kind of 'No way, leave me alone', but then when you
Lee:	I want Joe
Family therapist:	went back he told you
Dad:	Shut up
Family therapist:	When you're upset Nicky, what do you like people to
Lee:	I want to talk to Joe
Family therapist:	do if you're upset? What do you like people to do?
Dad:	He'll talk to you in a minute when he's finished (2006, 559–60).

After analysing a number of sessions with different families and therapists the research provides the following conclusions:

- Generally children in therapy are unsuccessful at taking the 'conversational floor' from an adult.
- There are many instances where children have to resort to interruptions as a tactic to gain space and, frequently, none of the adults permit this.
- Adults often ignore the child's potential contribution and mostly ignore any interruption from a child, and do not listen at all.
- Children's interruptions of conversation in therapy are not treated in a positive way.
- Children will attempt to interrupt adult speakers and are prepared to persist if necessary.
- Many interruptions are attempts by a child to change a topic, or to shift attention away from the immediate conversation topic.
- If the interruption is perceived by adults to be relevant to the adult's topic of conversation, then acknowledgement is more likely, but not always so (2006, 561–4).

The overall conclusions of the research are as follows:

- In family therapy the understanding is that all members should have equal rights to 'the floor', but that in actual therapeutic conversations children 'only have half membership'.

⇨

- Therapists need to give more space to children and be more aware that there are instances where children have to resort to interruptions as a tactic.
- Children are generally unsuccessful at taking the conversational floor from an adult in therapy and that it is, therefore, quite probable that this is the case in other institutional contexts.

Reflections on the research
Activity 1

The researcher, O'Reilly, says that within day-to-day talking assumptions about shared competence and status are often reflected in the way a conversation is conducted. What do you think the conversational excerpt reflects about assumptions about competence and status between the adults and the child?

Activity 2

The research says that examining children's own talk and their experience of others through conversations are ways of examining how children's worlds are constructed (2006, 551). What implications do you think the summary of the research findings might have in considering a child such as Lee's world, in terms of how he might see the ways adults and children relate to each other?

How do you think the research findings for children in family therapy might relate to Maskey's comment that 'priority is given to adult rather than children's voices, and . . . professional practice disenfranchises the child's representation of themselves'? What impact might this have on children's/a family's use of a health service such as family therapy?

Maskey's key points echo the earlier critique of the Bower et al.'s (2001) research findings. The prioritizing of the adult voice, and the often (not deliberate) collusion between adult health professionals and parent or carers, needs to change in order for children's health to be adequately attended to. This is a very practical illustration of the kind of impact of the problem identified in the analysis of Bower et al's review of research: of adult voices being prioritized over children's accounts.

There are many questions that can be developed from this critique. How can children's voices be heard? What does increasing children's participation in this way actually mean? What does research reveal about the impact of such ideas and practices? The following section explores these areas.

What ideas and practices have been developed concerning children's participation?

Kirby and Bryson (2002) identify a number of different ways in which children and young people can participate and be involved in processes such as decision making:

Table 7.1 Developed by Jones from Kirby and Bryson (2002, 10)

Participation	Description	Examples
One-off consultations	Express views and share experiences	Surveys Focus groups
Regular institutional or service provider process	Involvement in organizational decision making	School councils Students as researchers
Area-wide strategic	Input into development of local or national policy and practice	Council Youth Forum Social Action Groups
Integrated daily participatory approaches	Embedded daily ways of working between children and adults	Democratic schooling

The nature of such participation has been much discussed in recent research. The tensions within the relationships between participation, involvement, consultation and decision making features within research frameworks in this area. For example, Franklin and Sloper (2007) draw upon the Department of Health's (2002) distinction between participation and consultation. They refer to the Department's expectation that participation should go *beyond* consultation and 'ensure that children and young people initiate action and make decisions in partnership with adults, for example, making decisions about their care and treatment or in day-to-day decisions about their lives' (2002, 4). Cutler talks about Hart's (1992) ideas about participation, which see it as a hierarchy. At one end is being fully responsible for a process or aspect of one's life, at the other is providing information which others may choose whether to act on.

Cutler comments that such frameworks of participation are often seen as a ladder – with complete authority or full responsibility being at the top and consultation by providing information to others seen as a lower rung.

Key points: different levels of participation

This approach can be seen behind ways of looking at participation such as the four levels used by Alderson and Montgomery (1996) when defining children's participation:

1 Being informed.
2 Expressing views.
3 Influencing decisions.
4 Being the primary decider.

He makes a comment that is echoed by many of the research findings about children and young people's participation:

> We question this and would argue that both adults and young people find different levels of authority appropriate for different issues and in different situations.
>
> (2002, 2)

The idea here is that participation has many different facets and that the nature of children's engagement may be dependent upon factors such as age and development, or capacity for understanding and communication. Looked at in this way, seeing participation as a hierarchy is less relevant than seeing it as something that occurs as a process, dependent upon a number of different situational factors.

Participation and involvement: research and difference

Here issues concerning how other forms of disenfranchisement connect to issues concerning children being silenced. What does research reveal about whether factors such as gender, disability or race impact on children's participation? Researchers have pointed out to the comparative absence of engagement in research into certain aspects of children's lives and into the lives of certain children. Graham, for example, emphasized the importance of research bringing to the fore the diversity and differences of children and social experiences 'mediated through the social categories of race, gender and disability' (2007, 1306). She reviewed research outputs and points to the need for participatory approaches to research to redress 'the silencing and marginalization of black children in the wider society and the lack of qualitative research that documents their views and experiences' (2007, 1306). As an example of issues relating to such diversity and difference and the role of research in redressing this particular aspect of the silencing of children, the following will look at research that focuses on children, participation and disability.

Franklin and Sloper (2007) make the point that while, in general, children's participation is increasing, disabled children are less likely to be involved than non-disabled children. They refer in the policy context of their research to UNCRC Article 13, which states that a child shall have a right to freedom to seek, receive and impart information and ideas regardless of 'frontiers, either orally, in writing or in print, in the form of art, or through any other media of the child's choice' (United Nations, 1989, Article 13) and to the UK's Children's Act (2004), which reinforces *all* children's right to be listened to by service providers.

Their research aimed to identify factors supporting effective practice in involving disabled children. Case study work focused on areas such as the involvement of children in decision making about their own care within the review process, and in the use of processes such as youth forums in involving children in service development.

Example of research: disabled children's participation

The overall findings echoed many of the concerns and issues identified elsewhere in this chapter. The report says that participation of disabled children was 'fragile'. The research links this to its findings that the initiative and impetus of involving children in participation often rested on individuals, not on established organizational practices. Hence the research found that the actual practice of participation was adversely affected by the impact of an individual staff initiator's illness, staff turnover or by other organizationally established areas being given higher priority. The report comments that much of the participation that was identified was still not 'embedded in the culture of the organisation' and was conducted in 'isolation' rather than as part of general policies and procedures (Franklin and Sloper, 2007, x). While there was a general sense of the value of participation of children by those caring and working for them, the real meaning and 'impact of true participation

⇨

was less prevalent', as was the notion and practice of children being able to be involved at 'whatever level is appropriate to their ability' (2007, vii).

The research reported that children themselves viewed participation as a very positive experience. They:

- enjoyed the experience;
- felt validated by the process.

The research found that professionals tended to show confusion about what participation for disabled children could mean or involve. In part this concerned trying to engage with how children, such as those with learning impairments or complex communication needs, could be involved.

The research also found that these concerns related to 'children's competence, understanding and abilities to participate, coupled with unease about the interpretation of children's views' (2007, ix). A number of staff wrote about having to persuade parents or 'gatekeepers' of the need to involve children in decision making, or of being prevented from accessing the views of young people. Some of the respondents to the research reported facing attitudes that 'imply consultation cannot be made with individuals with limited communication skills', or staff being defensive feeling that 'the things that young people wanted to change were aimed at them' (2007, 62).

The report found that even where participation occurred, there was very little feedback given to children on the impact of their participation. Training and the time and skills to assist children in communication, for example, for those who do not use speech, was also a clearly identified need. The research did, however, discover some examples of changes being made to services as a result of children's input and to children having an impact within their own reviews.

Reflections on the research
Activity

The research reported that little feedback was given to children on their participation. Why do you think feedback might be considered to be important within the process of participation?

The research findings echo Cutler's ideas that, for some, children's participation is seen as a hierarchy. It illustrates that one of the possible impacts of this way of conceiving involvement is that if the adults do not see the participation as conforming with their ideas of what is 'adequate', then it does not matter. Hence, as the research pointed out, for some children engagement at levels appropriate to their developmental or communicative capacity might not be seen by staff or parents as 'counting'. In addition, the research indicates the need for staff and child alike to be given opportunities to develop their capacities to work together in participation.

Participation and involvement: rhetoric and reality

The World Bank has made the following points about young people. They:

- lack most of the processes through which adults can articulate their concerns;
- under the age of 18 are not allowed the right to vote in most countries;
- lack the power of the large commercial lobbies to influence government;
- lack access to media and the courts;
- are rarely members of trade unions or professional organizations that may negotiate on their behalf (Ishi, 2008).

It concludes that 'evidence does not support the claim that adults in either the public and private sphere always make decisions in the best interest of young people' (2008).

Protest to encourage natural drinks, India. Copyright Indranil Mukherjee/AFP/Getty Images

On the one hand this example illustrates the spread of ideas about involvement, that the language of children's participation is used by right-wing organizations such as the World Bank, as well as those with a left-wing or progressive ideology. However, whether rhetoric and reality actually meet, and actually bring benefit to children, is another matter. Over the past decade the rhetoric of participation and involvement for young people has become relatively widespread within new national polices in a number of countries, for example.

Youth Policy examples: India, Denmark, South Africa

India's 2003 *National Youth Policy* focuses upon empowerment in its list of 'Thrust areas of policy':

> 5.1 Youth empowerment: The Policy recognizes that in order for the youth to effectively participate in decision making processes, it is essential that they are better equipped with requisite knowledge, skills and capabilities.
>
> (India, 2003, 3)

Denmark's 1997 *National Youth Policy* is a parallel example. The intentions for this were that it should 'form an improved basis for young people's active participation in the development of democracy and their direct influence on and responsibility for matters affecting themselves' (Denmark, 1997). The nature of this participation is defined by its objectives. The following one clearly links to the idea of consultation:

'Updating and development of the youth policy shall be a dynamic process . . . youth policy shall, therefore, ensure that new knowledge about the living conditions and viewpoints of the young people is gathered on a continuous basis' (1997).

In the same year South Africa's National Commission also developed a *National Youth Policy* that involved bringing young people together (Mokwena, 2001). It includes ideas, similar to the Indian and Danish policies, such as:

- to provide a framework for youth development nationally, to ensure that youth are given meaningful opportunities to reach their full potential;
- to address the major concerns and issues critical to youth (2001, 70).

The reality behind such rhetoric can, however, be quite different from its surface, or apparent, commitment to participation and involvement. Mokwena draws on the situation in South Africa to comment on a wider phenomenon and problem:

It remains to be seen how the service programme will be implemented and if it does provide viable and meaningful opportunities for youth development. The danger of youth service programmes around the world (even when they work well) is simply that they can be used as a way of placating and containing youth.

(2001, 71)

He goes on to observe that, in many cases, the institutional framework required for promoting young people's participation and involvement in decision making and policy is very different from the frameworks that are in place for governments to *actually* design, implement and manage programmes and services. Undertaking participation is organized and carried out by one section or department of the government, but the actual making and implementing of decisions occurs in another. His conclusions are important for considering the research this chapter will go on to examine: that the structures for engaging young people in participation are clearly

not implementing bodies. Such structures have a role in shaping such interventions but they are not sufficient. The two are not mutually exclusive objectives, and the latter does not flow naturally out of the former. Representation does not equate delivery. There is evidence from other countries that suggests that such structures are used by government to contain youth dissent and thus do not have to bother to provide real opportunities. They serve to contain the main youth organisations and their leadership.

(2001, 72)

Key points from Mokwena's critique

- Is there an effective relationship between an institution's mechanisms for consultation and actual implementation?
- Does the representation or involvement serve as a container to keep children and young people quiet, rather than to listen to them?
- Does involving children and young people come from an institution's intention to change in response to what is found out, or is it only if this fits what adults want?

Mokwena very clearly foregrounds one of the issues key to reviewing research into children and young people's participation. This is, essentially, how, and whether, participation has an impact. It connects clearly to issues raised earlier that engage with power and attitudes towards children. What does research reveal about whether adult attitudes prevent children's participation leading from consultation to actual changes? If this is the case, does research offer any suggestions or solutions? What factors are identified as important in conducting and ensuring continuing involvement of children and young people?

How has research explored the practice and impact of children's participation in decision making?

Research was conducted by the Danish Youth Council into the Danish Government's 1997 youth policy, referred to earlier. The research investigated a three-year pilot project set up by the Danish Government aiming to advance the objectives of the youth policy. Specific efforts were made to involve as many young people as possible, including those who would not normally get involved in decision making. The range of participation activities and projects included:

- setting up youth councils;
- youth centres run by young people themselves;
- setting up peer counselling;
- appointing a team of reporters to pick up the wishes of local young people, co-operating with a local newspaper to set up a youth panel;
- appointing ombudsmen (Bach, 2000a).

Example of research: Danish youth participation research

The research findings (Bach 2000a, 2000b) show that young people had very different motives for wanting to participate. They did, however, make some discoveries about their participation and involvement.

> It is possible to say something about what generally motivates the young. The project has shown that young people have certain requirements in order to become and stay involved. These are:
> - personal challenge and satisfaction;
> - possibility for a dialogue concerning their visions and wishes;

⇨

Example of research—Cont'd

- transparent, realistic and reliable guidelines in relation to economy, time and politics;
- acceptance of new working methods, meeting and organization forms;
- to be part of the entire process;
- to have direct influence on both form and content; and to be able to turn ideas into reality within a short period of time.

(2000a, 2000b)

Young people evaluate project, UK Children's Fund (The South Tyneside Children's Fund gallery, UK, copyright and permission from The Children's Society. The project aims to help children and adults participate in identifying what services are needed to assist children in reaching their potential.)

⇨

Reflections on the research

Here we can see key themes that echo other research findings we have examined. These include:

- children and young people need to be involved throughout the process;
- the importance of dialogue;
- the process does not just involve adults receiving material from young people without response.

The idea of dialogue seems important as it means that children and adults actually engage with each other. The act of participation does not just involve consultation, with no adults responding after the act of consultation. Dialogue implies a critical and mutual engagement with ideas and practices and between adults and children. Another issue, present in the above list is highlighted by the summary of the enquiry. The research findings concluded that:

> Hardly any young people are keen on participating in projects that cannot be changed to accommodate their interests. In order for young people to get involved they require influence on content and working methods.
>
> (2000a, 2000b)

The researchers are emphasizing here the finding that in order for young people to get involved they require a genuine influence on what happens: that there is a response to their visions and wishes, and that the 'direct influence' of their work should be seen in an immediate way, in a 'short period of time'. Here, also, is a theme consistent with other research findings that stresses the importance of participation resulting in actual impact, and that this is seen by, and communicated to, the children and young people participating.

Activity

The earlier '**Key points from Mokwena's critique**' raises three main areas to pay attention to:

- Whether mechanisms for consultation are separate from those leading to actual implementation, and are powerless.
- Involvement as a container rather than genuine listening.
- Is there a real intention to change in response to what is found out, or is it only if this fits what adults want?

How do you think each of them relate to this summary of what the research in Denmark found out about young people's reasons for staying involved in participation?

⇨

Example of research: Penumbra – 'No harm in listening' (2001)

The research was part of a response to the lack of services in Edinburgh and its surrounding areas for young people (aged 16–21 years) who self-harm. Their definition of self-harm included cutting, overdosing and burning. The approach sought to gain young people's perspectives in a way that was rooted in ideas that challenge adult-centric provision. The brief for the research included two such key challenges:

- young people are rarely consulted with regards to the development of service provision or about the appropriateness of their own 'treatment plans' and 'support plans', which are provided by various statutory and non-statutory agencies.
- young people should be involved in the planning of appropriate services.

The result of this research work was the development of the *Edinburgh Self-harm Project* in 2005 funded by *Choose Life Edinburgh* to plug some of the gaps identified in service provision for young people who self-harm, their families and professionals involved in their care. This small-scale research was set up by the Scottish Executive's *National Programme in Improving Mental Health and Well-being* working with 'Penumbra', an organization working with people who self-harm. The research was commissioned and undertaken by independent researchers and it involved a study on the links between self-harm and suicide in young people. It took the form of one-to-one in-depth interviews with twenty young people aged 14–25 from across Scotland who had experience of self-harm and attempted suicide. The average age of starting self-harm was 12, the first suicide attempt was at 16.

The young people's participation enabled the research to find that young people had been in contact with a range of services, but that the professionals were not trained in recognizing or engaging with the young people in ways that they considered to be effective. For example:

- some existing services were viewed as judgemental and stigmatizing of young people who self-harmed.
- some professionals often use 'labels' and do not work with the young people to engage with the causes of self-harm, 'the symptoms are treated but the causes are ignored'.

The participation views of young people were made into specific recommendations designed to have an impact:

- Awareness of the issue of self-harm should be raised among staff as young people felt that having someone to talk to, whom they could trust, and who truly listened was one of the things that helped them most.

⇨

- Young people need privacy when their wounds are being treated at A&E, as being on public display can heighten their distress. Efforts should be made to provide a private room, or 'space' (i.e. cordoned off by a curtain) for a young person who has self-harmed.

In addition, changes to be implemented were clearly communicated to the young people by the project's findings and on their website, for example:

> As part of its focus on improving intervention with people at risk of self-harm or suicide, Scotland's Mental Health Delivery Plan has made a commitment to train 50% of key frontline healthcare professionals in using suicide assessment tools/suicide prevention programmes by 2010.
>
> *Source:* Penumbra Report (2003).

Reflections on the research
Activity

How does the summary of this research relate to the points made earlier about effective young people's participation?

- Children and young people being involved throughout the process.
- The importance of dialogue.
- The process should not just involve adults receiving material from young people without response and action.

Interview with Penumbra about their research

Maria Naranjo, Penumbra Self-Harm Services Co-ordinator
Phil Jones: **What do you feel is important about including young people's perspectives in this area?**

Maria Naranjo: Penumbra's ethos with regards work with young people is that they are the experts in their own lives. Therefore, from care plans to premises decoration, every detail has been carried out in consultation with service users to ensure empowerment and ownership. In addition, other opportunities have been provided to gain experiences of participation and consultation through, for example the '*See me*' *Campaign,* and *HeadsUp Scotland.* By providing accurate and meaningful information to parents/carers and friends, besides one-to-one support, it is possible to reduce the stress produced by self-harm within the relationship, empowering those who self-harm, their families and friends, to initiate an open dialogue about the issues surrounding self-harm.

Phil Jones: Are there any lessons you learnt, or things you feel are especially important about involving young people based on your experiences?

Maria Naranjo: Many young people who self-harm find themselves in a situation that puts their tenancy, accommodation, and social support, at risk. Self-harm is an issue that is not well understood and that raises emotions for people working with individuals who self-harm. There is evidence to point that the reaction of staff to whom the disclosure is made will have a massive impact in the ability of young people to reach out for help. Therefore, part of the projects' remit is to raise awareness and to provide ongoing consultancy service for professionals. Moreover, project workers work in partnership with other agencies involved in young people's care to maximize the quality of the service provided in consultation with the young people. Therefore, for Penumbra young people's participation is embedded in all levels of service development and service provision. Penumbra Self-Harm Services strived to facilitate Griesbach and Associates' research in an attempt to empower young people to help to shape services to accommodate their needs.

What does research say about the attitudes of parents and carers and professionals?

The previous section looked at individual pieces of research concerning children's exclusion from decision making, and on ways of responding to ideas about participation. The main parties involved within all the research have been the children and young people; professionals involved in services such as education, health and play; parents or carers and the researchers themselves. The following material looks at attitudes and children and young people's participation thematically, drawing on a variety of research findings.

Kirby and Bryson's research concluded that barriers to involving young people in area-wide strategic planning often lie in adult attitudes that create bureaucratic structures inaccessible to children, and that do not seek appropriate ways to find child-centred ways of communicating and giving feedback. They identify barriers as:

- formality, complexity, and bureaucracy;
- adult verbal and non-verbal communication being important for enabling or preventing young people's participation in making decisions;
- time constraints and output requirements acting as barriers;

- young people are not always being given feedback following their participation (2002, 5).

Mårtenson et al. (2007) in their review of findings indicate the importance of the child, parent or carer, and professional working together to create opportunities and develop participation. They concluded that:

- age-appropriate information and participation were prerequisites for allowing children to have possibilities of making competent decisions about their own care;
- children's decision-making competence is dependent on the attitudes of others, such as parents and healthcare professionals, and not only on their own capacity;
- perceived lack of competence does not exclude children from the human right to have a say;
- it should be noted that it is a decision, not an automatic necessity, to leave any decision making to a parent or healthcare professional.

(2007, abstract)

Franklin and Sloper (2007) said, in their findings, that actual experience altered held beliefs:

- When participation occurred, parents were able to find out from children what they thought about areas such as respite, and gained understanding of what their children enjoyed within service provision;
- After experiences of children's participation, many professionals realized they had underestimated the extent to which children could be involved, and the effect of using specific methods to assist participation and communication (2007, xi).

Their research identified areas that helped change held attitudes and practices. These drew on feedback from professionals reflecting on the process. The conclusions they considered as necessary to overcome or develop included:

- training in communication methods appropriate to engage with specific children in their case loads;
- training in how to consult children, especially where non-verbal methods were needed;
- time to undertake the work;
- senior management championing processes of participation and supporting practice;
- details of each child's method of communication recorded on case files to assist workers;
- participation being a core part of all process from simple choices on a child's likes and dislikes;
- appropriate ways of giving feedback to children on the outcomes of their participation, rooted in ways children could assimilate and engage with.

From I Can, You Can, We Can (UK's Knowsley Borough Council project 'I Can, You Can, We Can' innovating the use of visual arts, role and play in enabling children to express themselves and their ideas in order to become involved in developing the services that affect them.)

Spinetta et al. (2003) in their research have proposed a rights-based perspective that challenges held attitudes and practices. Their framework is for professionals to follow concerning decision making in medical matters. They conclude that: 'children clearly have a right to participate in medical decisions regarding their own treatment, based on the developmental level of the child' (2003, 244). The emergent guidelines from their research include:

- to share with the child developmentally relevant medical information specific to that particular child's health status
- to do so in the context of the child's own culture,
- to work with the child in a way that ensures he or she can actively participate in the decision-making process regarding his or her own health.

(2003, 244)

These guidelines challenge the attitude that only recognizes parents' legal rights in medical decision making. They differentiate the child's right to medical information and the parents' legal responsibility for the child. They acknowledge the responsibility, but say that this does not give them 'exclusive right over the child's health'. They advocate ways of encouraging the younger child's active participation in his or her own healthcare at an age-appropriate level of understanding. They suggest that for adolescents, there should be a full, and legally mandated, power to make their own decisions regarding medical treatment.

Bessell's (2007a) research into adult attitudes towards children's participation and competency in Filipino society describes a diverse, well-developed set of processes and structures, where each small community has a *Katipunan ng Kabataan* (youth assembly) with input into local and national policies and procedures. For example, in a situation where a child is removed from a situation of abuse, a child member of the council may be called on to accompany the child to the hospital of the police station (2007a, 10). Her interviews with officials working within the council for the welfare of children revealed that a commitment to children's participation needs to be developed across, and between, different departments. This is seen to be more effective than any initiatives being located in a children's 'silo'. Her work also revealed the central importance of departments jointly confirming clear, agreed ways of engaging with children's involvement. This concerned ways they involve children in decision making, for example, or the ways input from children will be acted upon: 'attitudinal barriers stem not only from concerns about the re-distribution of age-based power, but also from confusion and uncertainty about the ways in which participation occurs' (2007a, 12).

What does research say about the experiences of children and young people?

Graham and Bruce (2006) say that empowering children and young people through accessing and acting on their voice:

- allows children to communicate their social realities and experiences mediated through the social categories, of race, gender, disability;
- enables those living and working with children to engage with differences among children, rather than using reductive approaches that are based on sameness and generalities;
- creates access to children's accounts – these can help uncover the complex ways in which oppression and discrimination are having specific impacts on their lives and can help identify ways of engaging with barriers to equality, opportunities and well-being.

Kirby and Bryson concluded from their review that there is 'substantial evidence' that 'good participatory work benefits the participating young people, but that token involvement may not' (2002, 5). They report that changes in adult practices and attitude affect children's attitudes towards themselves. They state the benefits as:

- confidence;
- self-belief;
- knowledge;
- understanding and changed attitudes;
- skills;
- education attainment;
- having fun and making friends (2002, 5).

Franklin and Sloper's (2007) research echo these attitude shifts. It identified that children reported on participation having the following effects:

- felt included in what was happening around them;
- felt valued;
- experienced being listened to and being given attention;
- said they gained confidence;
- had fun (2007, xi).

Activities

The following activities are designed to help reflect back on some of the key concerns over the chapter as a whole.

Chapter activity 1

The language of much of the research findings about children's responses are largely to do with feelings about being listened to or involved, rather than satisfaction at having their voices acted on or satisfaction in seeing their suggestions, thoughts and experiences acted on and resulting in organizational change, for example. Why do you think this might be?

- What might the benefits for adults be of engaging with children's voices, of including them?
- What might the different organizational challenges be of the different levels of children and young people's participation?

Kirby and Bryson have said that we need to examine how systems can change to accommodate young people's participation, rather than expecting young people to participate in

⇨

predefined ways (2002, 6–7). Use the following structure to review two pieces of research in this chapter concerning children's participation. Look at the ways of working within the setting or settings and consider what you imagine the possible changes might involve from different angles. The first is based in Alderson and Montgomery's (1996) ideas:

Participation action initiated	Impact for organization structure and staff practice	Impact for child/ young person	Impact for parent /guardian
Children/Young people being Informed			
Children/Young people expressing views			
Children/Young people influencing decisions			
Children/Young people being the primary decider			

Chapter activity 2

In response to Maskey, Zenobia stressed in a letter in the BMJ the need of 'giving voices to children in medical systems' (2002, 599a). He goes on to look at how professionals can 'reveal children's experiences in relation to their family context' and looks at the idea of the child's voice being heard in the context of systems of communication (2002, 599a).

He says that 'Families offer the primary socialization for children. Parents are the first informal educators for children' (2002, 599a). He divides communication into positive and negative categories. A summary of his points are as follows:

Positive parent-child communication

- enhances children's good health;
- helps children express their health needs to their parents openly;
- helps parents give health knowledge to their children effectively.

Negative communication

- hinders children telling about their illness experience;
- blocks parents from delivering health knowledge to the children;
- is related to certain familial characteristics such as enmeshment, rigidity, over-protection and conflict-avoidance.

He advocates the need for the health professional to

- hear children's voices;
- be aware of the dynamics within a family to prevent the child being silenced or being presented as a symptom;
- understand the illness in the family-level as the first step;

⇨

Activities—Cont'd

- collaborate with the parents to enhance the child's expression of their experience (2002, 599a).

Looking back at the analysis of the Bowyer systematic review, in what ways might Zenobia's suggestions for prioritizing the child's voice in the family relate to the review summaries?

Summary

This chapter has:

- looked at how adult-centric ways of relating to children and young people can silence, disempower and harm them;
- examined ways in which a child-rights agenda challenges ideas and practices rooted in seeing children as not able to participate and take decisions;
- looked at the relationship between consultation, participation, decision making and impact in involving children and young people;
- reviewed research at a level of policy making to see how attitudes and practices can be changed in order to effectively involve children and young people;
- reviewed research within specific service situations to see how attitudes and practices can be changed in order to effectively involve children and young people.

Further reading

Children in Scotland (2003) 'Something to say', www.childreninscotland.org.uk/docs/participation/Somethingtosay.pdf.

A report on the Citizenship in Practice project run over two years, which aimed to develop and increase the participation of young people with disabilities in decision making. The project focused especially on young people with learning disabilities.

Kawaka Obbo, D. (2002) 'A report on young people's participation in public decision making in Uganda in empowering young people: the final report of the Carnegie Young People Initiative', London: Carnegie UK Trust.

A review of the system of consultation and representation of young people within the Ugandan political system. Looks at the formulation of the National Youth Policy and youth-driven initiatives and their impact on young people's lives.

Golombek, S. (ed.) (2002) 'What works in youth participation: case studies from around the world', International Youth Foundation.

Case studies from a number of different countries including the USA, India, the Philippines, Brazil, Germany and Thailand. The studies explore ways of working as well as tensions in working with participation within different political and social contexts.

Burr, R. (2004) 'Children's rights: international policy and lived practice', in Kehily, M. J. (ed.) *An Introduction to Childhood Studies*, Maidenhead: Open University Press.

Examines the UNCRC including the issue of participation rights. The chapter draws on research based on the author's fieldwork with children working on the streets or in reform school in Vietnam.

Research details

Parent's and children's voices in healthcare

Peer-reviewed journal. Bower et al. provide a systematic review of evidence concerning 'the effectiveness of interventions for child and adolescent mental health problems' (2001, 373). Researchers undertook the review in reference to the UK's National Service Framework's standards 1 and 2 and the commitment to the early identification of mental health problems, offering treatment for less severe problems and pursuing health promotion and problem intervention (NHS, 1999). Their review was through electronic databases and identified studies in sources such as the Cochrane Clinical trials Register (1999) and EMBASE (1980–99) as well as contacting experts in the field.

Bower, P., Garralda, E., Kramer, T., Harrington, R. and Sibbald, B. (2001) 'The treatment of child and adolescent mental health problems in primary care: a systematic review', *Family Practice*, 18, 373–82.

Researching children's interruptions

Peer-reviewed journal. O'Reilly (2006) investigated children in the institutional context of family therapy, drawing upon twenty-two hours of family therapy data and four families working with different therapists, using a qualitative approach to videotape analysis. Undertaken with ethical framework of the British Psychological Society.

O'Reilly, M. (2006) 'Should children be seen and not heard? An examination of how children's interruptions are treated in family therapy', *Discourse Studies*, 8, 549–66.

Disabled children's participation

Research by Franklin and Sloper (2007) aimed to identify factors supporting effective practice in involving disabled children. Case study work focused on areas such as the involvement of children in decision making about their own care within the review process, and in the use of processes such as youth forums in involving children in service development. The research was a combination of a UK national survey and case studies in six local authorities. It focused especially on children who are seen to have 'complex needs' (2007, viii) such as children with communication impairments, or with an autistic spectrum disorder.

Franklin, A. and Sloper, P. (2007) *Participation of Disabled Children and Young People in Decision-making Relating to Social Care*, University of York, Social Policy Unit

Danish Youth Participation Research

Bach's (2000) independent research conducted by the Danish Youth Council. Seventeen municipalities were chosen and given extra financial resources to develop new methods of youth participation. Certain stipulations were made such as young people having to be actively involved in the planning, realization and evaluation of the activities and initiatives.

Bach, T. (2000) 'Ung kommunalpolitik'. In *Når unge udfordrer demokratiet – dokumentation og debat*. (When the Young Challenge the Democracy – Documentation and Debate). Edited by Gritt Bykilde. Centre for Youth Research.

Penumbra 'No Harm In Listening'

Penumbra (2001) web summary, full report available from Penumbra. The research was commissioned and undertaken by independent researchers, Dawn Griesbach and Associates by Scottish Executive's National Programme in Improving Mental Health and Well-being working with 'Penumbra', an organization working with people who self-harm.

Penumbra Report (2003) www.penumbra.org.uk/young_people (copyright Penumbra 2003).

Challenging Otherness: child rights and the child's voice

8

Chapter Outline

Introduction and key questions

Children in many countries and within different cultures are living fulfilled lives. However, one of the threads running through this book is that significant numbers of other children experience life very differently. The pictures created by large- and small-scale research reveal complex situations typified for many as the shadow of the kind of lives many societies would aim for their children to have. The analysis of findings which have tried to name, and to understand, what is going wrong reveals interacting forces that create unhappiness and injustice for children. The chapters have examined the interplay between large-scale processes such as poverty, racism and sexism and their role in creating social exclusion and the macro processes of policy, law and national services provision. This book has also looked at the ways in which these and other more intimate processes are reflected in the daily encounters of children in their homes, the streets or in playgrounds. It has asked about the ways in which attitudes towards children are changing and *can* change

- How can attitudes be challenged?
- How can the child's voice be prioritized?
- What does research reveal about children's voices and their impact?

How can attitudes be challenged?

This book has explored the notion that certain attitudes and practices affect many children in ways that are not beneficial, and which harm or restrict them. It has also looked at how children in certain circumstances are affected by specific issues and attitudes – for example, the particular context of children living with family break up, or dealing with bullying or racism. The explorations into ideas of capability, fear, stereotyping or silencing have illustrated the ways in which attitudes run through these areas of children's living. The research analysed has illustrated the interwoven nature of policy and attitude, the ways adults and children in daily life create and react to each other with images and ideas: templates and transgressions of how they should and should not appear and act, what they can and cannot do. The language and actions of power and regulation held by adults in making and overseeing children's lives has been explored through the ways in which research, thinking and practice is enquiring about children in new ways.

The approach has been to examine how new questions have been formulated, driven by the increased attention to children's rights and lives.

In a way, there are two types of research that this book has drawn on. The first examined an aspect of children's lives, trying to gain a picture of what their lives are like and what forces are at play within their experiences. This has then been analysed and, where there are difficulties or problems, a reflection on why and how these occur is offered as well as ideas about challenge and change. The second type of research has focused more upon this area of change, exploring new way of living and working with children, and exploring children's responses, ideas and experience as new approaches, ideas and ways of working or living are attempted.

Within both types a number of threads within adult attitudes have been identified as problematic. These include seeing children according to long-held traditional views and stereotypes, adults holding onto their power and excluding children, and the idea of the othering of children.

The emphasis has been on identifying the ways these phenomena feature in the lives of children and adults, exploring how they operate and then to see how they can beneficially change.

The book has included numerous examples of the ways in which adults can relate to children as others. Table 8.1 (page 168) gathers themes from across the book, naming specific aspects of this process and linking them to adult attitudes and practices involving children. The third column of the table looks at how these are being challenged.

Within the third column a cluster of issues and stances become clear. These can be seen to form the core of the challenge to the processes of othering which this book has identified and explored through examples of research. One is that children's otherness, their difference, offers a challenge to adult-orientated norms of identity, and to contemporary ideas about key areas of social and cultural experience such as education, play, work and decision making. Another is an emphasis on children as active agents in their lives. Connected to this is the movement to enable children to change the ways they participate and have an impact in different areas of society: from government to home life. This table will be used in analysing the examples in the next section.

How can the child's voice be prioritized?

The different chapters in this book have offered an analysis of the different ways in which widely held attitudes have a negative effect on children's lives: from the notion that children are incapable, through to ideas that children are a threat. Each chapter has also offered material from research that is helping challenge negative attitudes and to see how different relationships with children can create positive experiences, outcomes and practices. Often these new directions have drawn on the United Nations Convention on the Rights of the Child and its concepts of protection, provision and participation. The following examples from research offer illustrations that adopt a 'rights-based approach' to the 'evolving capacities' of the child and the creating of environments to promote and respect children. They show how such approaches offer a challenge to practice that silences and makes the child 'other'. In a recent paper delivered at the Thomas Coram Research Institute, Moss referred to Cannela and Viruro in discussing otherness and children. He talked about the

Table 8.1 Overview of book: challenging othering, asserting difference

Process of othering	Adult othering children	Challenging othering asserting difference
Serves to mark and name those who are different from oneself	Adults mark childhood as a state of difference and this is used to disenfranchise and disempower children	Challenging laws, policies and practices that disempower and disenfranchise children
Stigmatizes those who are deemed to be 'different' from a group	Adults stigmatize children in terms of their deficits from adult-defined ideas of capability and maturity	Redefine ways of seeing and relating to children that emphasize children as capable and as developing capacities and abilities
Secures one's own identity by distancing others because of perceived differences	Adults reinforce their ideas of themselves as competent, able, caring and children as the shadow of this: incompetent, disabled, in need of care and immature	Redevelop relationships between adults and children that are based on mutuality and validation of parallels and differences, rather than the enforcement of difference
Reinforces majority notions of themselves as normal and others as deviant	Adult norms used to create standards and requirements in fields such as the law and education concerning judgement, behaviour and standards	The creation of child-centred and child-orientated systems of law, policy and practice
People who are seen and identified as other experience being marginalized, disempowered and excluded	Adults and the organizations they design are largely designed to serve and relate to adults and adult requirements, children's concerns are treated as invalid, not worthy of attention or inappropriately demanding	Address organizations' needs to develop in order to redress imbalance and that engage with children in their own right rather than as investments or mini adults
Behaving in daily interactions and using broader devices such as the law to re-inforce outsider status	From the macro level of national policies and laws to the micro level of family interactions children treated as the property of adults or as invisible to decision making	To involve and engage with children in ways that challenge and change organizational structures and ways of working to include children's voice and that create opportunities for the impact of the child's voice in ways of operating
Seeing others as in need of being managed or controlled by the majority because of their differences or deficits from the 'norm'	Adults create interpretations of children's development that focus on perceptions of inadequacy and deficits in areas such as judgement. These are used to emphasize adult ideas of vulnerability or of children and young people being incapable of valid judgement making or a danger to themselves or others and hence in need of care, regulation and control	Involve children at all levels of state, community and family processes and practice in ways that emphasize children as capable and stresses and develops their opportunities for decision making and empowerment
Opinions and experiences are not given value, they are silenced and excluded from being heard	Adults exclude children from having a voice in their own or others' experiences	To create opportunities for the child's voice to be developed, heard, valued and acted upon and to engage in dialogue

importance of listening and consulting children, but acknowledged that this is a complex process. Listening and consulting must take account of power relations and their inequalities between adults and children:

> When voice is 'conferred' upon 'the other' . . . without recognizing or attempting to alter the inequities that created the original distinctions, the 'giving of voice' or 'listening to' just becomes another colonizing apparatus.
> (Cannella and Viruro, in Moss 2002)

These examples are offered as a way of looking practically at such issues, about how to most effectively understand and respond to them in relation to communication, rights and power, and how to enable adults and children to communicate, work and live together to ensure rights are realized. The examples are followed by activities that invite connections to be made between them and the research and issues explored in the different chapters within this book.

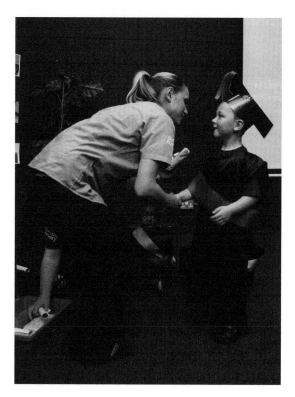

From Eureka! The National Children's Museum, UK

What does research reveal about children's voices and their impact?

The following are three examples of approaches which prioritize the voice of the child. They are included to help demonstrate some of the key responses to ways of challenging attitudes that silence children, see them as incapable, and exclude them from participation and decision making. They offer insight into ways of relating to children that see them as capable, competent agents involved in decision making and having opinions that count and that are acted upon.

Example of research: child researchers – understanding and exploring young carers from their perspective

This research was instigated by a young person, involving work with other 13- to 18-year-olds who are carers, and describes itself as:

- 'constructed entirely from a young person perspective'
- involving data collected 'young person-to-young-person' as this is different from 'adult-to-young person' as there are less 'power issues'
- using 'same peer language' as this improves understanding 'between one another in a way that is not possible for older researchers'
- 'a chance for young carers to voice their opinions away from the gaze of adults, thus adding to the richness of the data, and aim of achieving a better insight into the reality of young carers' (Tarapdar, 2007, 2).

The researcher sees this as reaching an understanding close to the reality of the young carers through semi-structured interviews.

The following are extracts from the findings:

> In the morning before I go to school, I wake up early, give him his medicine, and then go to school, then come back home and give him his medicine at five o'clock . . . and do the shopping for everyday stuff . . . then at night I have to lock the door and check, cos we have a big house, I have to check if there's anyone there.
>
> *Tom*

> I wash her up as she sometimes poos herself, I know its weird and stuff . . . I thought she was clued up, sometimes she's there and other times she isn't.
>
> *Tina*

> I have no one to turn to and that should be helped with. I have no safety net and no one to ask when I can't afford bread or bills.
>
> *David*

⇨

The researcher and young people engaged with things the carers felt needed attention.

Some carers felt embarrassed to disclose the full extent to which assistance was needed, others felt that their request was unworthy. There was a sense from the carers that they were not being seen by services:

> I mean they all just forget about you.
>
> *Julie*

> I had to ask people at the bus stop about getting transport for disabled people and getting disabled bus passes. It's like you don't exist.
>
> *Tom*

> I don't know who they are, what they do, cos no one comes to visit us.
>
> *Tom*

Some said that they needed help with the bureaucracy involved in caring:

> When I do apply for help, the forms are so long and hard to fill, I wish there was someone who would be able to help me with that.
>
> *David*

> No one tells you what to do or what you can do. It's ridiculous! There's so much shit to get through! Ooh don't get me started!
>
> *Katy*

They identified the need to raise the service providers' awareness of young carers support and the way carers' roles and support needs change over time: the 're-education of workers and agencies . . . so they remain up to date with the fluctuating nature of caring' (2007, 15–17).

The young researcher points out that the lack of awareness of young carers can be partly explained as caring is seen as an adult duty, so decision makers can be reluctant to define young people as young carers rather as 'helping mum and dad out' (2007, 18).

Reflections on the research
Activity 1

Within the research comment that its data collected 'young-person-to-young person' is different from adult to young person because of issues such as power and peer language.

Do you agree with this?

⇨

> ### Example of research—Cont'd
>
> ### Activity 2
>
> Do you think the idea and practice of children as researchers into their own lives relates to the earlier identified need to:
>
> > involve and engage with children in ways that challenge and change organizational structures and ways of working to include children's voice?
> >
> > (See Table 8.1)

Interview with Mary Kellett about the Children's Research Centre's approach to research

Dr Mary Kellett, Director, Children's Research Centre, Open University

Phil Jones: As an individual involved in the Children's Research Centre, how do you see your role as an adult?

Mary Kellett: My role as an adult is one of supporting, advising and empowering. I am there to transfer knowledge and skills so that children can design and lead their own research, not to judge whether the topics they choose are worthy of research or that the children are competent to undertake them. I see part of my role as trying to neutralize power relations wherever possible making sure children understand they are experts on their own lives and there is no reason why they can't be expert researchers with appropriate training. The empowering part is persuading children that they can make a unique contribution to the understanding of childhoods and children's lived experiences and help adults to better understand their needs, their values and their perspectives. It is important to provide children with comprehensive training so that they can make informed choices about their own research methods. Too often, in participatory research adults only teach children methods they have already decided on, putting significant adult filters in place from the outset. My guiding principle is to support not manage. I once asked a group of children I was working with how they would like my role to be defined. This caused some hilarity among them with one child suggesting I should be known as a 'research slave', another that I should be a 'research dogsbody' until we finally agreed that I could be a 'research assistant'. I felt rather flattered to be elevated to research assistant which rather sums up the dynamics of the power relations.

Phil Jones: **Issues concerning adult attitudes that allow participation, but deny any actual impact of children's involvement, is a theme within this book. How do you see the relationship in the Centre's work between participation and the actual impact of the children's research?**

Mary Kellett: I have quite strong views about this. Participation without influence or impact is sterile and is an insult to children's status and integrity. Sometimes tokenistic participation is used cynically to tick a political correctness box or to access funding without any intention of following through aspects that arise from children's involvement. At the Children's Research Centre (CRC) we work very hard to support children through the dissemination phase of their research to maximize the impact and influence of their research findings. This is where being a 'grown up' can help because, as adults, we can negotiate with adult gatekeepers to create opportunities for children's research voices to be heard. There are numerous examples of CRC children influencing outcomes through their research findings. Manasa Patil created quite a stir at the Department of Transport with her research study *Getting round as the child of a wheelchair user*. Ben Davies with his co-researcher Selena Ryan-Vig changed hearts and minds with their *Girls want to play too* study and succeeded in getting policy changed at local school level to extend the age for mixed gender football. To answer your question in simple terms, if there is no relationship between participation and outcome, then we are failing our child researchers. I would, however, add a note of caution about fuelling unrealistic expectations in children about the impact their research is likely to have since impact factors are more often about raising awareness rather than 'big bang' effects. In decades to come the child research movement (as by then it might be termed) is more likely to be viewed as a quietly undulating tide bringing children's agency gradually to adult shores rather than the crashing waves of a storm-fed revolution.

Example of research: children are experts in their own schooling

The following diagram represents the attitudes and tensions often experienced between adults and children within education systems:

⇨

Example of research—Cont'd

Accepting	PASSIVE	Indifferent
Conforming		Disengaged
POSITIVE		NEGATIVE
Enquiry		
Influencing taking responsibility		Rejecting
		Disaffected
	ACTIVE	

Diagram from McGregor (2005)

An emerging idea and area of practice is that students are experts in schooling and have insight into schools that adults do not, and can have different views on what is important. Work undertaken by innovators such as Reggio Emelio attempted to create a learning situation where 'the child is not seen as a passive recipient of education or care, but as an active participant' (Harker, 2005, 12). Some countries now make school councils mandatory, though, as identified earlier these can easily serve as lip service to the idea of children being involved and having effects on their education. McGregor has commented that to be successful this kind of approach demands:

> a real test of the climate of trust and respect, which is necessary for genuine
> enquiry and supported risk taking (McGregor, 2005, 27)

This attitude attempts to work against the kinds of oppositions represented by McGregor's diagram. The approach is to emphasize children's capability to be involved and to be given responsibility within the organizations they use.

The nature of this engagement with children as active agents within their own lives is seen to have important characteristics if it is to be successful. Fletcher's (2004) review highlights work in Washington that followed high school students co-creating the mission, guiding principles and co-writing the school constitution. The emphasis is on 'school-inclusive decision-making' that begins with all students in daily leadership classes, and their involvement in the architectural design of their school, reporting that much of their input was incorporated into the design and implementation of the school. Key points identified by Fletcher included:

- expanding common expectation of every student to become an active and equal partner in school improvement;

⇨

- instilling a core commitment within all members of the school community to meaningfully involve students as learners, teachers and leaders throughout the school;
- that schools have responsive and systematic approaches and engage in dialogue and this can be 'undermined by the disbelief of otherwise good-hearted adults who honestly believe they know what students think';
- that student perspectives and knowledge are not filtered with adult interpretations;
- the use of different aspects of participation – from school councils to peer-led action groups. The importance of role shifts in such participation: where teachers hear and negotiate with students, and are clear about acting and responding to what is said;
- that students are free to address wider questions, concerning areas such as the 'why' of learning, and are not confined to responses to implementing adult proposals about the day-to-day running of school life;
- that teachers and students are enabled to generate knowledge and insight together (2004, 8–13).

Fletcher identifies some of the potential downfalls within this approach including the danger of tokenism, in that issues which pupils are allowed to consider are carefully selected and that systems such as school councils can become a safety valve, not a true engagement involving decision making and representation with response in key areas of school life. In addition, he identifies the danger of creating a child elite of pupils whose voices may be more easily heard, or whom adults find it easier to engage with. So, for example, it may be very important for students who feel disengaged with school to be heard, but that they are not within the processes in place.

Fletcher concludes that 'teachers and learners . . . can move from the straitjackets which have historically bound their roles, to more open and inclusive relationships' (2004, 13).

Reflections on the research
Activity 1

How do you see the processes identified by Fletcher as relating to the ideas of:

- creating opportunities for the child's voice to be developed, heard, valued and acted upon and to engage in dialogue?
- practice that emphasizes children as capable and stresses and develops their opportunities for decision-making? (See Table 8.1)

Activity 2

McGregor's diagram can be used to identify tensions and difficulties in enabling children's meaningful engagement as decision makers within their own education – tensions between being 'passive' and 'active' learners, for example. McGregor talks of barriers to pupil engagement, such as a lack of confidence 'among both adults and young people (that) may result from existing power relations where students are

⇨

Example of research—Cont'd

too often seen as passive recipients of transmission practices in schools' and 'adult perceptions of young people as being unable to take responsibility' along with the anxiety of teachers to open up their practice to scrutiny and students to develop trust to take part in dialogue and change (McGregor, 2005, 4–7).

What factors in creating an environment for this to occur does the research identify?

Example of research: getting sorted – young people as healthcare experts and innovators

Webster's (2007) work researched approaches to involving young people with diabetes. It deliberately challenged many of the adult attitudes analysed in this book. It actively tried to avoid health approaches where:

- services are developed for a child or young person and are determined by other people;
- problems associated with young people are seen by professionals 'as a burden';
- young people are seen as an 'object of concern, care, and not a citizen with rights' (2007, 12).

The research involved fifteen schools with forty-one young people aged 12 to 17 taking part. The work involved researching and creating 'a programme written for young people, by young people' (Webster, 2006 in 2007).

It aimed to respond to demand for need and effectiveness and to enhance children and young people's knowledge, skills and confidence to self-manage. In addition, it sought to empower young people through the self-management of the impact of their condition on their well-being and health. The initiative involved young people in the aims, design and implementation of the research and that young people 'be involved and retain control of the process' (2007, 14). Focus group interviews, or 'talking groups' as the young people referred to them, were used and the data helped create the content and delivery of a model for self-care (2007, 14). The perspective came from the young people themselves, and they were free to explore and elaborate on their own ideas and experience. This became the content of 'an expert patient programme' named as 'Getting Sorted' self-care

⇨

programme. Young people were recruited as facilitators for the workshops that resulted and the idea that the self-management courses could be best run by those with personal experiences (2007, 19).

Commentary from the young people included:

- makes a change to be listened to
- first time I have had a chance to talk about how I feel – don't usually have people to talk to at school
- felt safe to talk about parents, school, clinic.

(2007, 35)

- understand condition within my life
- get to see the steps involved.

(2007, 36)

The research report emphasizes the importance of the involvement of young people in analysing the data, 'as young people gave their own perspective they analysed and categorized the data differently from the research team using their own language' (2007, 40). The process had direct results on healthcare and practice. An innovative self-care model written by young people for young people was designed and implemented with impact on young people with diabetes.

Reflections on the research
Activity 1

How do you see the processes within this research as relating to the ideas of:

- involving and engaging with children in ways that challenge and change organizational structures and ways of working to include children's voice and that create opportunities for the impact of the child's voice in ways of operating?

(See Table 8.1)

Activity 2

How do you consider the following ideas in relation to Webster's work with the children?:

- that children can offer a different perspective on processes involved in healthcare from adults
- that children can take responsibility for aspects of their health
- it redefines ways of seeing and relating to children that emphasize children as capable and as developing capacities and abilities.

(See Table 8.1)

An emerging agenda

The impetus of much research and practice, such as these three examples, informed by the new sociology of childhood, can be seen as an emerging agenda:

- to see and understand the ways adults and children interact – from national levels of policy to life in the home and street;
- to look at what is helpful and what is harmful to both children and adults within these relationships;
- to redress the negative impact of adult attitudes such as stereotyping;
- to redress power imbalances and processes that have silenced and excluded children;
- to find ways to inform, include, empower and enable children;
- to value children's agency and voice;
- to engage with the ways children's agency and areas such as children's rights will change society;
- to work to see what changes need to be made, and how they can be made, as a result of children's agency.

The impetus is fuelled by critiques of many ways of seeing children, and is informed by new images. However, if looked at in this way, the most important thing about the new sociology of childhood becomes less about the establishing of new images, and more about finding processes which arise from, and drive, children's and adults' demands for change in attitudes and action. These concern children's empowerment as active agents in their own and others' lives.

Children's Society Young Tenants Support Project (The Young Tenants Support Project, UK, copyright and permission from The Children's Society. The project works to equip young people at risk of being on the streets with the life skills for independent living.)

Activities

The following activities are designed to help reflect back on some of the key concerns over the book as a whole.

The activities take some of the ideas within Table 8.1 and trace them across the book. Each one is designed to link the three examples of research in this chapter back to different key parts of the book.

Activity 1: Chapter 3 – Othering

Chapter 3 contained the idea that public policy in many countries talks about children's rights to provision, protection and participation. It noted a shift towards the concept of the participation by children and young people being valued as a basic principle and the importance of their voice being heard, but that in many 'social exclusion policies are directed at young children, yet their voice is rarely heard' (Hill et al., 2004, 82)

In what ways do you see the work of the three research examples contributing to the ideas of hearing young people's voices in arenas where they were previously unheard?

Activity 2: Chapter 4 – Competence

Chapter 4 challenged ideas of children that start from the idea that they are inadequate and incompetent, and looked at ways of viewing and working with children that saw them in terms of their competence and as active and engaged in decisions about their lives.

The chapter looked at ideas that challenged the vicious circle of adult expectations creating few opportunities for children to be engaged and involved. In services for children this included:

- assessing child-based outcomes that include and prioritize children's as well as adult's perceptions;
- asking children directly for their views in ways that are sensitive to each child's capacity:
- gaining a better understanding of children's conceptualization of particular areas such as health and illness, which will help resolve some of the legal and ethical debates about whether children of different ages and intellectual abilities can give informed consent.

The chapter's findings emphasized the importance of:

- respecting children's desire to be informed;
- creating appropriate and specially developed information sources and appropriate ways of delivering material to increase children's ability to participate competently in decision making;
- using methods which complement written and verbal material that relate to children's use of images, or play to absorb, and engage with, information.

How do you see the three examples of research in this chapter relating to enabling children to be informed? How do they help gain insight into children's perspectives and experiences? How do they prioritize children's perceptions and ideas?

⇨

Activities—Cont'd

Activity 3: Chapter 5 – Stereotyping

This chapter's examination of stereotyping looked at the way it can have negative effects on children. It emphasized the importance of engaging with children as individuals, rather than relating to them in terms of generalized stereotypes based on adult preconceptions.

The research notes that:

- socialization pressures to act in accordance with stereotypes can have negative impact;
- these come from many different sources such as parents, teachers and peers;
- they comment on the 'prescriptive nature of stereotypes . . . accordingly children are motivated to act in accordance with stereotypes' (Serbin et al., 2001, 7–8);
- it is important to engage with difference, and be sensitive to children's individual ideas, needs and ways of developing.

How do you see the research examples engaging with the issue of avoiding stereotyping and being committed to the importance of engaging with individual children's experiences?

How do you see the work challenging stereotypes that adults may hold, based on lack of insight into the actual lives of children?

Activity 4: Chapter 7 – Participation

Graham and Bruce (2006) say that empowering children and young people through accessing and acting upon their voice:

- allows children to communicate their social realities and experiences mediated through the social categories, of race, gender, disability;
- enables those living and working with children to engage with differences among children, rather than using reductive approaches that are based on sameness and generalities;
- creates access to children's accounts – these can help uncover the complex ways in which oppression and discrimination are having specific impacts on their lives and can help identify ways of engaging with barriers to equality, opportunities and well-being.

How do you see the three research examples relating to children communicating their own realities and experiences? How do you see the work in relation to these ideas of the importance of engaging with differences and identifying barriers to opportunity and well-being?

Summary

This chapter has:

- explored how adult attitudes can be challenged, by examining a range of ideas and looking at children's input;

- examined research into initiatives that look at different, practical ways of involving children;
- looked at positive ways in which children's voices be prioritized;
- explored the different areas considered within this book, and drawn conclusions from the different strands of research in order to reveal different ways of rethinking childhood, and adult attitudes towards children;
- reviewed the research within this book to identify the impact children's voices can have in different areas of society.

Further reading

Kellett, M. (2005) *How to Develop Children as Researchers.* London: Paul Chapman.

A review of approaches and issues in enabling children to become researchers. It includes material on ethics, framing research questions, methodology, communicating results and the nature of the role of children as active researchers.

Prout, A., Simmons, R. and Birchall, J. (2006) 'Reconnecting and extending the research agenda on children's participation: mutual incentives and the participation chain', in Kay, E., Tisdall, M., Davis, J. D., Prout, A. and Hill, M. (eds) *Children, Young People and Social Inclusion: Participation for What?* Bristol: Policy Press.

Examines the development of children's participation in different arenas and looks at issues concerning motivation, resources, the nature of opportunities for participation and the dynamics of the process.

Research details

Child researchers – understanding and exploring young carers from their perspective

This research was instigated by a young person, involving work with other 13- to 18-year-olds who are carers (Tarapdar, 2007). This was part of the work of the Open University's Children's Research Centre where children design and run their own research projects.

Tarapdar, S. (2007) '"I don't think people know enough about me and they don't care": Understanding and exploring the needs of young carers from their perspective'. Children's Research Centre, Open University. http://children's-research-centre.Open.ac.uk/research.

Children are experts in their own schooling

The nature of this engagement with children as active agents within their own lives is seen to have important characteristics if it is to be successful.

Fletcher's review highlights work in Washington that followed high school students co-creating the mission, guiding principles and co-writing the school constitution (Fletcher, 2004).

Fletcher, A. (2004) *Stories of Meaningful Student Involvement*. Washington: Sound Out.

Getting sorted – young people as healthcare experts and innovators

Webster's (2007) report on work involving young people living with a long-term condition developing a research project that drew on a qualitative survey of the views and young people's experiences of living with a long-term condition. The approach used planned focus group interviews and workshops.

Webster, E. (2007) 'Development and evaluation of the "Getting Sorted" Self Care Workshops for Young People with Diabetes'. Report. Leeds Metropolitan University, Bradford and Airedale Teaching Primary Care Trust.

References

Alanen, L. (2001) 'Childhood as a Generational Condition: Children's daily Lives in a Central Finland Town', in L. Alanen and B. Mayall (eds) *Conceptualizing Child-Adult Relations*, London: Routledge/Falmer Press, pp. 129–43.

Alderson, P. (1993) 'European Charter of Children's Rights', *Bulletin of Medical Ethics*, 92, 13–15.

Alderson, P. and Montgomery, J. (1996) *Healthcare Choices: Making Decisions with Children*. London: Institute for Public Policy.

Anderson, S., Bromley, C. and Given, L. (2005) 'Public attitudes towards young people and youth crime in Scotland: findings from the 2004 Scottish Social Attitudes Survey'. Scottish Executive Education Department.

Anderson, S., Ingram, D. and Hutton, N. (2002) 'Public attitudes towards sentencing and alternatives to punishment'. Scottish Parliament Paper 488. Online: www.scotland.gov.uk/Resource/Doc/55971/0015628.pdf.

Appleton, P., Pritchard, P. and Pritchard, A. (1988) 'Evaluation of a 12 month in-service course for health visitors in behavioural intervention method with infants and pre-school children'. Unpublished manuscript.

Aynsley-Green, A. (2005) Children's Commissioner cited at ESRC Information centre. Online: www.esrc.ac.uk/ESRCInfoCentre.

Bach, T. (2000a) 'Ung kommunalpolitik'. In Når unge udfordrer demokratiet – dokumentation og debat. (When the Young Challenge the Democracy – Documentation and Debate). Bykilde, G. (ed.). Centre for Youth Research.

Bach, T. (2000b) 'Erfaringer fra ungdomskommuneforsøget, 1. halvår 2000'. ('Experiences from the project of Youth Municipalities, first half of the year 2000') Danish Youth Council. Online: www.duf.dk

Badham, B. (2004) 'Participation – for a change: disabled young people lead the way', *Children and Society*, 18, 2, 143–54.

Baker, S. L. (2004) 'Pop in(to) the bedroom', *European Journal of Cultural Studies*, 7, 1, 75–93.

Batahala, L. (2008) 'Intergroup relations: when is my group more important than yours?' ACTA Digital Comprehensive Summaries, Uppsala Faculty of Social Sciences, 38.

Bell, J. (1997) 'Understanding adultism: a key to developing positive youth-adult relationships'. Online: http://freechild.org/bell.

Bessell, S. (2007a) 'Adult attitudes towards children's participation in the Philippines, policy and governance'. Discussion papers. Crawford School of Economics and Governance, Australian National University. Online: www.crawford.anu.edu.au.

Bessell, S. (2007b) 'Children, welfare and protection: a new policy framework?' in MacIntyre, A. J. and McLeod, R.H. (eds) *Indonesia, Democracy and the Promise of Good Governance*. Singapore: Institute of Southeast Asian Studies, 138–59.

Bhaba, H. K. (1994) *The Location of Culture*. London & New York: Routledge.

Bluebond-Langner, M. (1978) *The Private Worlds of Dying Children*. Princeton, NJ: Princeton University Press.

BMRB (British Market Research Bureau) (2004) *CAFCASS Client Satisfaction Survey*. London: BRMB.

Bolzan, N. (2008) '"Kids are like that!" Community attitudes to young people', report to the National Youth Affairs Research Scheme, Commonwealth, State and Territory Government of Australia. Online: www.facs.gov.au/internet/facsinternet.nsf/aboutfacs/programs/youth-kids_that.htm.

Bower, P., Garralda, E., Kramer, T., Harrington, R. and Sibbald, B. (2001) 'The treatment of child and adolescent mental health problems in primary care: a systematic review', *Family Practice*, 18, 373–82.

Boyland, M. (2007) 'Attitudes towards street play, ICM research for Playday 2007: our streets too!' Online: www.playscotland.org/pdfs/ AttitudesTowardsStreetPlay2007.pdf.

Buckingham, D. (2004) 'New media, new childhoods? Children's changing cultural environment in the age of digital technology', in Kehily, M. J. (ed.) *An Introduction to Childhood Studies*. Maidenhead: Open University Press.

Burr, R. (2004) 'Children's rights: international policy and lived practice', in Kehily, M. J. (ed.) *An Introduction to Childhood Studies*, Maidenhead: Open University Press.

Byron, T. (2008) 'Safer children in a digital world: the report of the Byron review'. Online: www.dfes. gov.uk/byronreview (accessed June 12 2008).

Cannella, G. S. and Viruro, R. (2004) *Childhood and Postcolonization*, London: Taylor and Francis.

Carnegie Young People Initiative (2008) 'Empowering young people: final report of the Carnegie Young People Initiative'. Online: Cypi.carnegieuktrust.org.uk/cypi.final_report.

Cawson, P., Wattam, C., Brooker, S. and Kelly, G. (2000) *Child Maltreatment in the United Kingdom*. London: The National Society for the Prevention of Cruelty to Children.

Children in Scotland (2003) 'Something to say'. Online: www.childreninscotland.org.uk/docs/ participation/Somethingtosay.pdf.

Children's Bureau (2006) 'Child welfare outcomes 2002–2005: report to Congress'. Child Welfare Information Gateway. Online: www.acf.hhs.gov/programs/cb/pubs/cwo05/index.htm.

Children's Bureau (2008) 'Child maltreatment 2006: summary of key findings, numbers and trends'. Child Welfare Information Gateway. Online: www.acf.hhs.gov/programs/cb/pubs/cm06/index.htm.

Children's Rights Alliance and National Society for the Prevention of Cruelty to Children (2007) *You feel Like You're Nothing: The UN Study on Violence Against Children*. London: Children's Rights Alliance and National Society for the Prevention of Cruelty to Children.

Children's Rights Development Unit (1994) 'UK agenda for children: a systematic analysis of the extent to which law, policy and practice in the UK complies with the principles and standards contained in the UN Convention on the Rights of the Child'. CDRU publication.

Children's Society (2007) *Learning and Me, Good Childhood Evidence Summaries, The Good Childhood, A National Enquiry*. London: The Children's Society.

Childwatch (2006) 'Understanding and contextualizing children's real participation, submission to committee on The Rights of the Child Day of General Discussion', September 2006, Childwatch International Research Network. Online: www.childwatch.uio.no/projects/Citizenship/Childwatch %20submission_CRC%20Day%20of%20General%20Discussion.pdf.

Cornerstone Consulting Group (2001) 'Communities and youth development coming together'. Report.

Council of Europe (2005) Report by Alvaro Gil-Robles, Commissioner for Human Rights, CommDH 6, 8 June Strasbourg.

Coverley, C., Garralda, M. and Bowman, F. (1995) 'Psychiatric Intervention in primary care for mothers whose schoolchildren have psychiatric disorders', *British Journal of General Practice*, 45, 235–7.

Cutler, D. (2002) 'Taking the initiative – promoting young people's involvement in public decision making in the USA'. Report. Carnegie UK Trust.

Das Dasgupta, S. (1998) 'Gender roles and cultural continuity in the Asian Indian immigrant community in the US in sex roles', *A Journal of Research*, June, 1–9.

Davies, B. (2005) 'Threatening youth revisited: youth policies under New Labour'. The encyclopaedia of informal education. Online: www.infed.org/archives/bernard_davies/revisiting_threatening_youth.html.

Davis, L. and Kirkpatrick, G. (2000) *The EURIDEM Project: A Review of Pupil Democracy in Europe*. London: Children's Rights Alliance for England.

De Castro, L. (2004) 'Otherness in me, otherness in others: children's and youth's constructions of self and other', *Childhood*, 11, 4, 469–93.

Denmark (1997) *National Danish Youth Policy*. Online: www.uvm.dk.

Department for Children, Schools and Families (2008) *Fair Play: A Consultation on the Play Strategy*. London: Department for Children, Schools and Families and Department for Culture, Media and Sport.

Department for Education and Skills DfES (2003) 'Working together: giving children and young people a say', consultation document, DfES publications. Online: www.dcsf.gov.uk/consultations/downloadableDocs/239_2.pdf (accessed May 21 2008).

Department of Health DOH (2001a) 'Seeking consent: working with children'. Online: www.dh.gov.uk/en/Publicationsandstatistics/Publications/PublicationsPolicyandGuidance/DH_4007005 (accessed 21 May 2008).

Department of Health DOH (2001b) 'Consent what you have a right to expect – a guide for young'. Online: www.dh.gov.uk/en/Publicationsandstatistics/Publications/PublicationsPolicyAndGuidance/DH_4005202 (accessed 21 May 2008).

Department of Health (2002) *Listening, Hearing and Responding*. London: Department of Health.

Deutsch, F. M. (2007) 'Undoing gender', *Gender and Society*, 21, 1, 106–27.

Devine, D. (2002) 'Children's citizenship and the structuring of adult-child relations in the primary school', *Childhood*, 9, 3, 303–20.

Dixon-Woods, M., Young, B. and Heney, D. (1999) 'Partnerships with children', *British Medical Journal*, 319, 778–80.

Dowty, T. (2008) 'DNA databases: fuelling children's criminality?', *childRIGHT*, cR, 246, 18–21.

Duckett, P. S., Sixsmith, J. and Kaga, C. (2008) 'Researching pupil well-being in UK secondary schools: community psychology and the politics of research', *Childhood*, 15, 1, 89–106.

Eden, K. (2000) 'Let's go Euro', *International Journal of Advertising and Marketing to Children*, 2, 1, 83–93.

ESCR collective paper (2004) 'Setting the agenda: social inclusion, children and young people', *Children and Society*, 18, 97–105.

Fenstermaker, S. and West, C. (eds) (2002) *Doing Gender, Doing Difference*. New York: Routledge.

Fielding, M. (2004) 'Transformative approaches to student voice: theoretical underpinnings, recalcitrant realities', *British Educational Research Journal*, 30, 2, 295–311.

Finney, J., Lemanek, K., Cataldo, M., Katz, H. and Fuqua, R. (1989) 'Pediatric psychology in primary healthcare: brief targeted therapy for recurrent abdominal pain', *Behaviour Therapy*, 20, 283–91.

Finney, J., Riley, A. and Cataldo, M. (1991) 'Psychology in primary healthcare: effects of brief targeted therapy on children's medical care utilisation', *Journal of Pediatric Psychology*, 16, 447–61.

Fletcher, A. (2004) *Stories of Meaningful Student Involvement*. Washington: Sound Out.

Forrester, M. A. (2002) 'Appropriating cultural conceptions of childhood: participation in conversation', *Childhood*, 9, 255–76.

France, A. (2007) *Understanding Youth in Late Modernity*. Milton Keynes: Open University Press.

Franklin, A. and Sloper, P. (2007) 'Participation of disabled children and young people in decision-making relating to social care'. University of York, Social Policy Unit.

Gardner, R. (2008) 'Developing an effective response to neglect and emotional harm to children'. University of East Anglia and The National Society for the Prevention of Cruelty to Children.

Gask, L. and Usherwood, T. (2002) 'ABC of psychological medicine: the consultation', *British Medical Journal*, 324, 1567–9.

Golombek, S. (ed.) (2002) 'What works in youth participation: case studies from around the world', International Youth Foundation.

Graham, M. (2007) 'Giving voice to black children: an analysis of social agency', *British Journal of Social Work*, 37, 1305–17.

Graham, M. and Bruce, E. (2006) 'Seen and not heard: sociological approaches to childhood: black children, agency and implications for child welfare', *Journal of Sociology & Social Welfare*.

Grove, N. J. (2006) 'Our health and theirs: forced migration, othering and public health', *Social Science and Medicine*, 62, 1931–42.

Hardy, M. and Armitage, G. (2002) 'The child's right to consent to x-ray and imaging investigations: issues of restraint and immobilization from a multidisciplinary perspective', *Journal of Child Healthcare*, 6, 2, 107–19.

Harker, L. (2005) 'Lessons From Reggio Emilia', *Guardian*, 11 November, 11–12.

Hart, R. (1992) *Children's Participation from Tokenism to Citizenship*. Florence: UNICEF.

Hawton, K., Rodham, K. with Evans, E. (2006) *By their Own Young Hand – Deliberate Self-harm and Suicidal Ideas in Adolescents*. London: Jessica Kingsley Publishers.

Hemrica, J. and Heyting, F. (2004) 'Tacit notions of childhood: an analysis of discourse about child participation in decision making regarding arrangements in cases of parental divorce', *Childhood*, 11, 4, 449–68.

Henderson, M. (2007) 'At last, science discovers why blue is for boys but girls really do prefer pink', *The Times*, 21 August. Online: www.timesonline.co.uk/tol/news/uk/science/article2294539.ece.

Hill, M. and Tisdall, K. (1997) *Children and Society*. London: Prentice Hall.

Hill, M., Davis, J., Prout, A. and Tisdall, K. (2004) 'Moving the participation agenda forward', *Children and Society*, 18, 77–96.

Holland, J., Reynolds, T. and Weller, S. (2007) 'Transitions, networks and communities', *Journal of Youth Studies*, 10, 1, 97–116.

Holland, S. and O'Neill, S. (2006) 'We had to be there to make sure it was what we wanted: enabling children's participation in family decision-making through the family group conference', *Childhood*, 13, 1, 91–111.

Hough, M. and Roberts, J. V. (2003) 'Youth crime and youth justice: public opinion in England and Wales'. The Nuffield Foundation and the Institute for Criminal Policy Research.

Hough, M. and Roberts, J. V. (2004) *Youth Crime and Youth Justice*. Bristol: The Policy Press.

Huffaker, D. A. and Calvert, S. L. (2005) 'Gender, identity and language use in teenage blogs', *Journal of Computer-Mediated Communication*, 10, 2, article 1.

Hurlbert, A. and Ling, Y. (2007) 'Biological components of sex differences in colour preference', *Current Biology*, 17, 16, R623.

India (2003) *National Youth Policy*. Online: www.yuva.nic.in/downloads/NATIONALYOUTHPOL-ICY2003.doc.

Ishii, I. (2008) 'Youth advisory groups – new allies in the World Bank's work', Human Development Network Children and Youth Department Working Paper, No. 6. Online: http://web.worldbank.org/WBSITE/EXTERNAL/TOPICS/EXTCY/Participation.

James, A., Jenks, C. and Prout, A. (1998) *Theorizing Childhood*. Cambridge: Polity Press.

Jarvis, P., Brock, A. and Brown, F. (2008) 'Three perspectives on play', in Brock, A., Doods, S., Jarvis, P. and Olusoga, Y. (eds) *Perspectives on Play*. Harlow: Pearson.

Joiner, L. (2003) 'The student's voice', *American School Board Journal*, 190, 1. Online: www.asbj.com/2003/01/0103coverstory.html (accessed 21 May 2008).

Jones, R. M., Taylor, D. E., Dick, A. J., Singh, A. and Cook, J. (2007) 'Bedroom design and decoration: gender differences in preference and activity', *Adolescence*, Fall, 1–10.

Kane, E. (2006) '"No way my boys are going to be like that!" Parents' responses to children's gender nonconformity', *Gender and Society*, 20, 149–76.

Kawaka Obbo, D. (2002) 'A report on young people's participation in public decision making in Uganda in empowering young people: the final report of the Carnegie Young People Initiative', London: Carnegie UK Trust.

Kehily, M. and Montgomery, H. (2004) 'Innocence and experience: a historical approach to childhood and sexuality', in *An Introduction to Childhood Studies*. Maidenhead: Open University Press.

Kellett, M. (2005) *How to Develop Children as Researchers*. London: Paul Chapman.

Kemshall, H. (2008) 'Risks, rights and justice: understanding and responding to youth risk', *Youth Justice*, 8, 1, 21–38.

Kilkelly, U. (2008) 'Youth courts and children's rights: the Irish experience', *Youth Justice*, 8, 1, 39–56.

Kirby, P. and Bryson, S. (2002) *Measuring the Magic? Evaluating Young People's Participation.* London: Carnegie Young People's Initiative.

Kriecbergs, U., Vladimarsdottir, U., Onelov, E., Henter, J. I. and Steineck, G. (2004) 'Talking about death with children who have severe malignant disease', *New England Journal of Medicine*, 351, 12, 1175–86.

Krisberg, B. and Marchionna, S. (2007) 'Attitudes of US voters toward youth crime and the justice system', *Focus*, February, 1–8.

Kroenke, K. (2002) 'Psychological medicine', *British Medical Journal*, 324, 1536–7.

Lansdown, G. (2005) 'The evolving capacities of the child'. UNICEF and Save the Children.

Leonard, M. (2007) 'Trapped in space? Children's accounts of risky environments', *Children and Society*, 21, 432–45.

Lewis, C. C., Pantell, R. H. and Sharp, L. (1991) 'Increasing patient knowledge, satisfaction and involvement: randomized trial of a communication', *Pediatrics*, 88, 2, 351–8.

Livingstone, S. (2005) 'UK children go online: end of award report'. London School of Economics and Political Science. LSE Research online.

Livingstone, S. and Bober, M. (2005) 'UK children go online: final report of key project findings'. London School of Economics and Political Science. LSE Research online.

Lyon, T. D. (1995) 'Assessing children's competence to take the oath: research and recommendations', *American Professional Society on the Abuse of Children Advisor*, 9, 1, 3–7.

MacNaughton, G., Hughes, P. and Smith, K. (2007) 'Young children's rights and public policy: practices and possibilities for citizenship in the early years', *Children and Society*, 21, 458–69.

Madge, N. (2006) *Children These Days.* Bristol: Policy Press.

Mantle, G., Leslie, J., Parsons, S., Plenty, J. and Shaffer, R. (2006) 'Establishing children's wishes and feelings for family court reports', *Childhood*, 13, 4, 499–518.

Mårtenson, E. K., Astrid, R. N. and Fägerskiöld, M. (2007) 'A review of children's decision-making competence in healthcare', *Journal of Clinical Nursing*, 10, 1365.

Martin, K. (2005) 'William wants a doll. Can he have one? Feminists, child care advisors, and gender-neutral child rearing', *Gender and Society*, 19, 4, 456–79.

Maskey, S. (2002) 'Children are still seen but not heard', *British Medical Journal*, 325, 599.

McNamee, S., James, A. L. and James, A. (2003) 'Can children's voices be heard in family court proceedings? Family Law and the construction of childhood in England and Wales', *Representing Children*, 16, 187–96.

McNeish, D. (1999) 'Promoting participation for children and young people', *Journal of Social Work Practice*, 13, 2, 191–203.

MENCAP (2006) 'Bullying wrecks lives: the experiences of children and young people with a learning disability'. Report MENCAP.

Mesie, J., Gardner, R. and Radford, L. (2007) *Towards a Public Service Agreement on Safeguarding.* London: Department for Education and Skills, National Society for the Prevention of Cruelty to Children.

Messner, M. (2000) 'Barbie versus Sea Monsters: children constructing gender', *Gender and Society*, 14, 765–84.

Mokwena, S. (2001) 'Deepening democracy: meeting the challenge of youth citizenship', in Foster, J. and Naidoo, K. (eds) (2002) *Young People at the Centre. Participation and Social Change*. London: Commonwealth Secretariat.

Moss, D. (2008a) 'Children who offend', in Jones, P., Moss, D., Tomlinson, P. and Welch, S. (eds) *Childhood: Services and Provision for Children*. Harlow: Pearson.

Moss, D. (2008b) 'The Social Divisions of Childhood', in Jones, P., Moss, D., Tomlinson, P. and Welch, S. (eds) *Childhood: Services and Provision for Children*. Harlow: Pearson.

Moss, P. (2002) 'From children's services to children's spaces'. Paper ESRC Seminar, Challenging 'Social Inclusion'.

Moss, P. (2005) 'Listening to children: beyond rights to ethics'. Thomas Coram Institute. Online: www.Itscotland.org.uk/earlyyears (accessed 4 February 2007).

Moss, P. and Petrie, P. (2002) *From Children's Services to Children's Spaces: Public Policy, Children and Childhood*. London: Routledge.

Nairn, A. and Griffin, C. (2006) 'The Simpsons are cool but Barbie's a minger: the role of brands in the everyday lives of junior school children'. Report. University of Bath.

Nairn, A., Griffin, C. and Gaya Wicks, P. (2006) 'Beckham: Hero, villain or a bit of both? The children's viewpoint'. Report. University of Bath.

Nairn, A., Ormrod, J. and Bottomley, P. (2007) 'Watching, wanting and wellbeing: exploring the links'. National Consumer Council.

National Health Service (1999) *National Service Framework for Mental Health: Modern Standards and Service Models*. London: HMSO.

Norman, J. (2004) 'Survey of teachers on homophobic bullying in Irish second-level schools'. Dublin City University. Online: http://www.belongto.org/article.aspx?articleid=30.

NSPCC Online: www.nspcc.org.uk/Inform/resourcesforprofessionals/Statistics/ChildProtectionRegisterStatistics/childprotectionregisterstatistics_wda48723.html.

NSPCC, Key statistics, NSPCC inform. Online: www.nspcc.org.uk/Inform/resourcesforprofessionals/Statistics.

O'Donohoe, S. and Bartholomew, A. (2006) 'The business of becoming: children, consumption and advertising in transition, child and teen consumption 2006', paper no. 37. Online: www.cbs.dk/content/download/41857/616432/file/.

O'Loan, S., McMillan, F., Motherwell, S. (LGBT Youth Scotland) and Bell, A., Arshad, R. (2006) 'LGBT Youth research report on how homophobic incidents and homophobia is dealt with in schools'. University of Edinburgh. Online: www.scotland.gov.uk/Publications/2006/05/25091604/0.

O'Reilly, M. (2006) 'Should children be seen and not heard? An examination of how children's interruptions are treated in family therapy', *Discourse Studies*, 8, 549–66.

Observatório de Educacão (2006) 'LGBT – Relatório sobre Homofobia e Transfobia (report on homophobia and transphobia), by rede ex aequo – associação de jovens lésbicas, gays, bissexuais, transgéneros e simpatizantes', Lisbon. Online: http://www.ex-aequo.web.pt/arrioquivo/observato/OE2006.pdf.

Office of National Statistics (2006) 'Permanent and fixed period exclusions from schools and exclusion appeals in England, 2004/2005'. Online: www.dcsf.gov.uk/rsgateway/DB/SFR/s000662/index.shtml.

Oliver, C. and Candappa, M. (2003) 'Tackling bullying: Listening to the views of children and young people'. Department for Education and Skills Research Report RR400, p. 44.

Owusu-Bempah, K. (2005) 'Race, culture and the child', in Hendrick, H. (ed.) *Child Welfare and Social Policy*. Bristol: Policy Press.

Penumbra Report (2003) Online: www.penumbra.org.uk/young_people.

Peter, J. and Valkenburg, P. M. (2007) 'Adolescents' exposure to a sexualized environment and notions of women as sex objects', *Sex Roles*, 56, 381–95.

Pierson, J. (2001) *Tackling Social Exclusion*. London: Routledge.

Pomerleau, A., Bolduc, D., Malcuit, G. and Cossette, A. (1990) 'Pink or blue: Environmental gender stereotypes in the first two years of life', *Sex Roles*, 22, 359–67.

Prout, A., Simmons, R. and Birchall, J. (2006) 'Reconnecting and extending the research agenda on children's participation: mutual incentives and the participation chain', in Kay, E., Tisdall, M., Davis, J. D., Prout, A. and Hill, M. (eds) *Children, Young People and Social Inclusion: Participation for What?* Bristol: Policy Press.

Qvortup, J. (2004) 'Editorial: the waiting child', *Childhood*, 11, 3, 267–73.

Radford, L. and Hester, M. (2006) *Mothering Through Domestic Violence*. London: Jessica Kingsley Publishers.

Raymond, L. (2001) 'Student Involvement in School Improvement: from data source to significant voice', *Forum*, 43, 2, 58–61.

Reay, D. and Lucey, H. (2000) 'Children, school choice and social differences', *Educational Studies*, 26, 1, 83–100.

Redmond, G. (2008) 'Child poverty and child rights: edging toward a definition', *Journal of Children and Poverty*, 14, 1, 63–82.

Renold, E. (2002) 'Presumed innocence', *Childhood*, 4, 415–34.

Rheingold, H. L. and Cook, K. V. (1975) 'The contents of boys and girls' rooms as an index of parents' behaviour', *Child Development*, 46, 2, 459–63.

Rights of Us: Children & Young People in England (2005) Online: www.uwe.ac.uk/solar/ChildParticipationNetwork/.

Royal College of Paediatrics and Child Health (2002) *Good Medical Practice in Paediatrics and Child Health: Duties and Responsibilities of Paediatricians*. London: Royal College of Paediatrics and Child Health.

Runeson, I., Martenson, E. and Karin, E. (2007) 'Children's knowledge and degree of participation in decision making when undergoing a clinical diagnostic procedure', *Pediatric Nursing*, November, 1–7.

Schildkrout, E. (1978) 'Age & gender in Hausa society: socio-economic roles of children in Urban Kano', in la Fontaine, J. S. (ed.) *Sex and Age as Principles of Social Differentiation*. London: Academic Press.

Scotland's Commissioner for Children and Young People (2007) 'Adults' attitudes towards contact with children and young people'. Report Scotland's Commissioner for Children and Young People and Rocket Science.

Serbin, L. A., Poulin-Dubois, D., Colburne, K. A., Sen, M. G. and Eichstedt, J. A. (2001) 'Gender stereotyping in infancy: visual preferences for and knowledge of gender stereotyped toys in the second year', *International Journal of Behaviour Development*, 25, 7–15.

Shield, J. P. H. and Baum, J. D. (1994) 'Children's consent to treatment', *British Medical Journal*, 308, 1182–3 (7 May).

Spinetta, J., Masera, G., Jankovic, M. and Oppenheim, D. (2003) 'Valid Informed consent and participative decision-making in children with cancer and their parents: a report of the working party on psychosocial issues in pediatric oncology', *Medical and Pediatric Oncology*, 40, 4, 244–6.

Spivak, G. C. (1985) 'Can the subaltern speak?', in Barker, F. (ed.) *Europe and its Others*. Colchester: University of Essex.

Spring, J. (1994) *Wheels in the Head: Educational Philosophies of Authority, Freedom, and Culture from Socrates to Paulo Friere*. New York: McGraw-Hill.

Stainton Rogers, W. (2004) 'Promoting better childhoods: constructions of child concern', in Kehily, M. J. (ed.) *An Introduction to Childhood Studies*, Maidenhead: Open University Press.

Sutton-Smith, B. (2005) *Play: An Interdisciplinary Synthesis*. Lanham: University Press of America.

Svoboda, J. S., Van Howe, R. S. and Dwyer, J. C. (2000) 'Informed consent for neonatal circumcision: an ethical and legal conundrum', *Journal of Contemporary Health Law & Policy*, 17, 61–133.

Tarapdar, S. (2007) 'I don't think people know enough about me and they don't care: understanding and exploring the needs of young carers from their perspective'. Children's Research centre, Open University. Online: http://childrens-research-centre.open.ac.uk/research.cfm.

Teachernet (2008) 'Working together: listening to the voices of children and young people'. Online: www.teachernet.gov.uk/wholeschool/behaviour/participationguidance/ (accessed 21 May 2008).

Thomas, T. (2007) 'A year of tackling anti-social behaviour: some reflections on realities and rhetoric', *Youth and Policy*, 94, 5–18.

Thorne, B. (1987) 'Re-visioning women and social change: where are the children?', *Gender and Society*, 1, 1, 85–109.

Thorne, B. (2002) 'From silence to voice: bringing children more fully into knowledge', *Childhood*, 9, 3, 251–4.

Tomlinson, P. (2008) 'The politics of childhood', in Jones, P., Moss, D., Tomlinson, P. and Welch, S. (eds) *Childhood: Services and Provision for Children*. Harlow: Pearson.

Tornay-Purta, J., Lehmann, R., Oswald, H. and Schulz, W. (2001) *Citizenship and Education in Twenty Eight Countries*. IEA: The International Association for the Evaluation of Education and Achievement.

Turner, J. C. and Reynolds, K. J. (2004). 'The social identity perspective in intergroup relations: theories, themes, and controversies', in M. B. Brewer and M. Hewstone (eds) *Self and Social Identity*. Oxford: Blackwell.

UK's Children's Act (2004) Online: www.opsi.gov.uk/acts/acts2004/ukpga_20040031_en_1.

UK's Crime and Disorder Act (1998) and the Anti-Social Behaviour Act (2003)

UNCRC (2007) 'Committee on the Rights of the Child, forty fourth session', Geneva, 15 January–2 February. Online: www.crin.org/docs/CO_K_44.pdf.

UNICEF (2001) 'Young voices poll'. Online: www.unicef.org/newsline/01pr42.htm.

UNICEF (2007) 'Child poverty in perspective: an overview of child well-being in rich countries', Innocenti Report card 7, UNICEF Innocenti research centre, Florence, United Nations Children's Fund.

United Nations Convention on the Rights of the Child (1989) Online: www.unhchr.ch/html/menu3/b/k2crc.htm.

Varichon, A. (2006) *Colors: What They Mean and How to Make Them*. New York: Abrams.

Verkaik, R. (2005) 'The ASBO generation', *Independent*, 20 June.

Walker, G. (2008) 'Safeguarding children: visions and values', in Jones, P., Moss, D., Tomlinson, P. and Welch, S. (eds) *Childhood: Services and Provision for Children*. Harlow: Pearson.

Ward, L. M. and Friedman, K. (2006) 'Using TV as a guide: associations between television viewing and adolescents' sexual attitudes and behavior', *Journal of Research on Adolescence*, 16, 133–56.

Warwick, I., Chase. E. and Aggleton, P. with Sanders, S. (2004) 'Homophobia, sexual orientation and schools: a review and implications for action'. Department for Education and Skills Research Report RR594.

Weare, K. and Gray, G. (2003) 'What works in developing children's emotional and social competence and wellbeing?' Department of Education and Skills Research Report No 456.

Webster, E. (2007) 'Development and evaluation of the "Getting Sorted" Self Care Workshops for Young People with Diabetes'. Report. Leeds Metropolitan University, Bradford and Airedale Teaching Primary Care Trust.

Weis, L. (1995) 'Identity formation and the process of "othering": unravelling sexual thread', *Educational Foundations*, 9, 17–33.

Welch, S. (2008) 'Childhood – rights and realities', in Jones, P., Moss, D., Tomlinson, P. and Welch, S. (eds) *Childhood: Services and Provision for Children*. Harlow: Pearson.

Weller, S. (2007) 'Sticking with your mates? Children's friendship trajectories during the transition from primary to secondary school', *Children and Society*, 21, 5, 339–51.

West, C. and Zimmerman, D. H. (1987) 'Doing gender', *Gender and Society*, 1, 2, 125–51.

Whyte, B. (2003) 'Young and persistent: recent developments in youth justice policy and practice in Scotland', *Youth Justice*, 3, 2, 74–85.

Wilensky, D. (2007) 'Putting its princesses to work, global license!' June 15, 2. Online: www.licensemag.com/licensemag/article.

Wright, J. (2001) 'Treating children as equals', *New Renaissance Magazine*, 8, 3, 27–8.

Zenobia, C. C. Y. (2002) 'Children should be heard in their family context', *British Medical Journal*, 325, 599.

Index